NORTH ISLAND
weekend tramps

SHAUN BARNETT

CRAIG
POTTON
PUBLISHING

For Tom and Lee and the tramps we'll do together

Design: Robbie Burton
Maps: Geographx, Wellington, New Zealand
Printed by Everbest Printing Co. Ltd, China

Craig Potton Publishing
98 Vickerman Street, PO Box 555, Nelson, New Zealand
www.craigpotton.co.nz

First printed in 2002
Reprinted 2004

© Craig Potton Publishing
© Text and photographs: Shaun Barnett/Black Robin Photography
ISBN 0-908802-89-7

ACKNOWLEDGEMENTS

The idea for this book originated with Rob Brown, my co-author on *Classic Tramping in New Zealand*. Rob suggested there was a need for guidebooks on weekend length tramps, and Craig Potton Publishing approached me with the idea of writing one for the North Island. Another friend, Nick Groves, has written a companion volume for the South Island.

I'd like to thank a number of people who were great companions in the hills while I researched this book, namely Daryl Ball, Angela Barnett, Melissa Booth, Rob Brown, Rachel Bryce, Dave Campbell, Andy Dennis, Margot Ferrier, John Fitzgerald, Tony Gates, David Hall, Dave Hansford, Kirk MacGibbon, Debbie Hoare, Stephen Hormann, Andrew Lynch, Sarah-Jane Mariott, Neil McLennan, John Ombler, Darryn Pegram, Rick Porras, Bruce Postill, Jane Reeves, Jim Ribeiro, Jason Roxburgh, Mark Schwarz, Tania Stanton, Louise Thornley, Hayden Titchener and Anaru Waa. A number of the above also provided helpful comments on the drafts.

Department of Conservation (DoC) staff from all over the North Island have been exceedingly helpful in checking draft chapters. In particular, I'd like to thank Andy Bassett, Wayne Boness, Kevin Connell, Brian Dobbie, Nick Doney, Michele Elborn, Isaac Emmett, Warren Geraghty, Geoff Harris, Stephen Hormann, Simon Mailer, Jon Maxwell, Bruce Postill, Ray Scrimgeour, Pat Sheridan, Steve Sutton, Eddie Te Kahika, Mark Townsend, Gavin Walker and Don Woodcock. I must also acknowledge the many pamphlets DoC produces on various tracks, which proved an excellent source of information.

CONTENTS

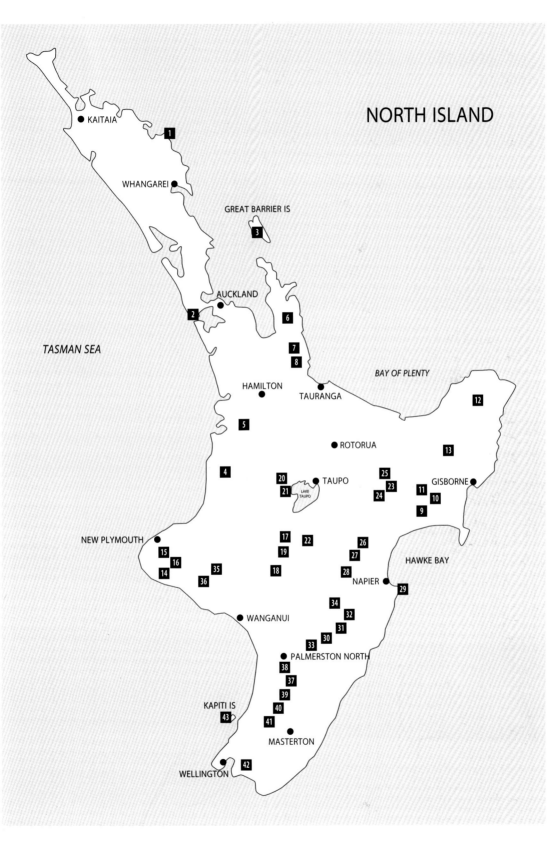

NORTH ISLAND

TASMAN SEA

BAY OF PLENTY

HAWKE BAY

KAITAIA

WHANGAREI

GREAT BARRIER IS

AUCKLAND

HAMILTON

TAURANGA

ROTORUA

TAUPO

LAKE
TAUPO

GISBORNE

NEW PLYMOUTH

NAPIER

WANGANUI

PALMERSTON NORTH

KAPITI IS

MASTERTON

WELLINGTON

INTRODUCTION

While many people look to the South Island for tramping trips, in a number of ways the North Island offers a greater range of experiences for trampers. Certainly the diversity of forests and the presence of volcanic landscapes distinguish North Island tramps from those on the 'mainland'. Another advantage of North Island tramps is the generally low numbers of sandflies – something that certainly cannot be said of the South Island! Furthermore, the majority of New Zealanders do indeed live in the North Island, and aside from their annual leave are left with only weekends in which to head for the hills.

This guidebook is intended for trampers who are looking for ideas and information on a range of weekend-length tramps in the North Island. I've taken the liberty of including two longer tramps, primarily because of their popularity as 'long weekend' trips, especially at Easter. Aside from these (the Matemateaonga Walkway in Whanganui National Park and the Lake Waikaremoana circuit in Te Urewera National Park), most of the remaining tramps described can be accomplished by moderately fit trampers over the course of a normal weekend. A few of the harder trips do require a very good level of fitness if they are to be completed in two days, although they can more easily be tackled over three.

Tramps in this book have been chosen from the length and breadth of the North Island, reflecting a range of terrain, natural history and level of difficulty. Included are tramps in the kauri forests of the Coromandel, Great Barrier Island and the Kaimai Range; and coastal walks at Cape Brett in Northland, Auckland's Waitakere Ranges and Cape Kidnappers in Hawkes Bay. The majestic podocarp forests of Whirinaki and Pureora are unique to the North Island, while volcanic landscapes also provide distinctly North Island tramping experiences – this book includes tramps at Mt Taranaki and Tongariro National Park.

Several of the tramps include a chance to climb the highest peak in an area: Kaweka J in Kaweka Forest Park, Mangaweka in Ruahine Forest Park, Mt Manuoha in Te Urewera National Park, Mt Hikurangi in Raukumara Forest Park, Mt Matthews in Rimutaka Forest Park, Mitre in Tararua Forest Park and Mt Taranaki in Egmont National Park. Yet others follow historic routes, including the Waitawheta Valley and Pinnacles Hut tramps, as well as the Matemateaonga Walkway. While on all of the tramps you'll encounter a range of native animals and birds, experiencing rare and interesting wildlife is a particular feature of both the Kapiti and Cape Kidnappers tramps.

A high proportion of the tramps cross a mixture of terrain, passing through bush, crossing rivers and ascending tops. Some of the walks are very well known, including the Tongariro Crossing, Southern Crossing and Lake Waikaremoana. Others are less well known, and several have never before featured in tramping guidebooks, notably the Leitch's Clearing, Cape Brett, Waihaha Hut and Waioeka Forest walks.

LENGTH AND DIFFICULTY

Each tramp is classified according to difficulty, which readers should note depends very much on conditions. Wet weather could very well turn a medium river trip into a hard one, while winter snow may transform a medium or hard tops trip into one that requires mountaineering skills. When selecting a tramp it is also important to take the abilities of all party members into consideration.

Each walk is classified into 'easy', 'medium', 'hard' or 'mountaineering' grades. On an 'easy' walk you can expect gentle terrain, well-marked tracks, few if any river crossings, and walking times of less than three to four hours per day. On a 'medium' trip you may have river crossings, and there could be steep sections of track or some travel on unmarked, open tops. Travel times could be five to six hours per day. A 'hard' tramp will involve longer days, possibly eight hours or more, and is likely to feature some unmarked travel and considerable river crossing.

Only one 'mountaineering' trip is included in this book: the ascent of Taranaki. While in summer this can be a simple scree climb, in most other seasons tackling Taranaki will require some mountaineering knowledge, as well as the use of an ice axe and crampons. However, by far the majority of the tramps fall into the easy and medium categories, with just a few in the hard category.

Where appropriate, options for either shortening or lengthening tramps have been suggested, allowing for changes in weather and varying levels of fitness. For example, the Sunrise Hut tramp can be spread over two longer days when a traverse of Te Atuaoparapara to Waipawa Forks Hut is undertaken, or simply accomplished as a daytrip just to the hut itself.

KEEPING INFORMATION UP TO DATE

Although every effort has been made to ensure that information in this guide is both correct and up to date, please remember that wild places change constantly. Floods alter rivers, volcanoes erupt from time to time and storms can devastate forests. Furthermore, the condition of tracks and huts varies according to how recently they have been maintained. For these reasons, it is advisable for trampers to check with local Department of Conservation (DoC) offices for updates. The relevant DoC telephone number has been given for each tramp.

MAPS

Each tramp in this book is accompanied by a simple map, largely to help the reader follow the track description. The maps indicate tracks, huts, bridges and major topographical features, but are not intended to be used for navigation – for this you should purchase a NZMS 260 series 1:50,000 topographical map. Details of the correct map(s) for the tramps are included in the 'fact file' at the beginning of each chapter. Note that true left refers to the left bank of a river when facing downstream, and true right to the right bank.

-------	Track described	++++	Railway tracks	) (	Saddle	↓↓	Swamp
··········	Route only	▲	Mountain	\\	Falls	🔵63	State Highway
- - - - -	Additional tracks	)(	Foot bridge	///	Dam	ℹ️	Information Centre
··········	Additional route	♠	Hut	⋈	Bridge		
————	4 Wheel Drive tracks	▶	Shelter/Bivvy	♠	Cave		
- - - -	Mountain bike track	♠	Campsite	◣	Tunnel		

HUTS AND HUT FEES

New Zealand's hut network – which includes over 1000 backcountry huts – is perhaps unique in the world, but requires your support if it is to be maintained. DoC charges modest fees for most huts, excepting Basic Huts/Bivvy (Category 4) which are free. Charges per person per night for other huts are Great Walk Huts (Category 1): $10 – $40; Serviced Huts (Category 2): $10; Standard Huts (Category 3): $5. Each category roughly relates to facilities provided. Most Great Walk huts have heating and gas cooking facilities. Serviced Huts are more basic and may not have heating or cooking facilities, but are likely to have an indoor sink and running water. Standard Huts usually just have mattresses and perhaps a woodstove or open fire. Basic Huts/Bivvy may be just a simple shell, without even mattresses. Hut tickets can be purchased from most DoC offices and from some information centres.

For those doing a lot of tramping (say, spending more than 10 nights in a backcountry hut per year), a good-value option is to purchase a Backcountry Hut Pass. These cost $90 adult and $45 youth and enable you to use all Serviced and Standard Huts. It would pay to check with DoC for up-to-date information on hut fees and for bookings.

HUT ETIQUETTE

At night or during bad weather, the hut forms the focus of the tramping experience and is part of the tradition of the New Zealand backcountry. A few simple courtesies make the experience an enjoyable one for all, even in a crowded hut.

Always make room for newcomers, even if the hut is nearing capacity. When the hut is full, consider using a tent if you have one. Inside, keep your gear tidy and contained, and try not to spread out too much. Remove wet boots before entering the hut to keep the floor clean and dry. Cook with ventilation. When leaving, make sure all benches and tables are clean, sweep the floor, close all windows and doors, and ensure you've replaced any firewood used. You won't go far wrong if you follow the rule, 'Leave the hut as you'd hope to find it'.

WATER AND CONSERVATION

Giardia is present in many backcountry waterways, but there are still significant areas where you can safely drink straight from the stream. If in doubt, carry water treatments, boil the water for five minutes or use a water filter.

Do not use soap or detergent in lakes or streams, and where possible use toilets. If there is no longdrop, go to the toilet at least 100 metres from water sources and bury your waste in a shallow 'cat scrape'. When camping take care not to pitch your tent in a fragile area, and refrain from hacking poles out of saplings.

Have consideration for the environment: don't take away anything natural and don't leave anything unnatural. Carry out all your rubbish and any you find. Avoid lighting fires when they are unnecessary (in summer) or during a fire ban. In some areas (such as the bushline) dead firewood is in very short supply and should be burned only when absolutely necessary. Dismantle outdoor fireplaces after use.

SAFETY AND EQUIPMENT

There is not the scope in this book to give a detailed description of equipment and safety, but a brief list of what should be carried for a typical weekend tramp is as follows: sleeping bag, billy, burner, fuel, warm woolly hat, sunhat, gloves, raincoat, warm jersey or fleece, two pairs of polypropylene or woollen long-johns, two wool or polypropylene tops, a pair of shorts, first-aid kit, mug, plate, utensils, two pairs of warm socks, map, compass, sunscreen, candles, matches and enough food for the duration of the trip plus a few extra snacks and one extra meal. For some trips you might like to take a tent, or at least a flysheet and sleeping mat. In winter, you may need to add ice axe, crampons, sunglasses, more warm gear, extra fuel and food.

You should leave your intentions, including possible bad-weather alternatives, with a trusted friend who can, in the event of your party becoming overdue, be relied upon to contact the Police Search and Rescue. Remember that rivers are the biggest hazard in the backcountry and cause the most deaths. You should therefore be well versed in the current Mountain Safety Council river-crossing techniques and have practised these before you need to use them in a real situation. Many tramping clubs offer introductory courses to river crossing, bushcraft and navigation.

Finally – happy tramping!

REFERENCES AND FURTHER READING

Armitage, D. (ed.) *Great Barrier Island* (Christchurch: Canterbury University Press, 2001)

Barnett, S. & Brown, R. *Classic Tramping in New Zealand* (Nelson: Craig Potton Publishing, 1999)

Bates, Arthur P. 'The Waitotara Valley, a few background notes' from *The Wanganui Tramper*, issue Oct–Dec (1989)

Dawson, J. & Lucas, R. *Nature Guide to the New Zealand Forest* (Auckland: Godwit, 2000)

Dreaver, A. *An Eye for Country – the Life and Work of Leslie Adkin* (Wellington: Victoria University Press, 1997)

Gibbons, A. & Sheehan, G. *Leading Lights, Lighthouses of New Zealand* (Christchurch: Hazard Press, 1991)

Greenaway, R. *The Restless Land – Stories of Tongariro National Park* (Turangi: DoC/ Tongariro Natural History Society, 1998)

Groves, N. *South Island Weekend Tramps* (Nelson: Craig Potton Publishing, 2003)

Maclean, C. *Tararua – The Story of a Mountain Range* (Wellington: Whitcombe Press, 1994)

Maclean, C. *Kapiti* (Wellington: Whitcombe Press, 1999)

Ombler, K. *National Parks and Other Wild Places of New Zealand* (Cape Town: Struik New Holland Publishers, 2001)

Potton, C. *Classic Walks of New Zealand* (Nelson: Craig Potton Publishing, 2004)

Spearpoint, G. *Waking to the Hills* (Auckland: Reed-Methuen, 1985)

NZ Wilderness is a monthly magazine that regularly features weekend tramps, as well as stories on conservation, exploration, mountain biking, sea kayaking, climbing and natural history.

Trampers on the Whanahuia Range, Ruahine Forest Park

Cape Brett Scenic Reserve

Duration: 2 days.

Grade: Medium.

Times: Rawhiti to Deep Water Cove Track Junction: 4–6 hours. Junction to Cape Brett Hut (21 bunks, gas cookers, Category 2): 2–3 hours. In the future, DoC may build a hut at Deep Water Cove.

Map: Q05 Bay of Islands.

Access: From Paihia, drive to Opua and catch the car ferry, then drive east to Rawhiti and Oke Bay. The track begins at a signpost in Oke Bay. Cape Brett Hut is locked with a combination keypad, and you must pre-book a bunk with DoC. In addition, the first part of the walk crosses private land administered by Cape Brett Walkways Ltd, and there is a track maintenance fee of $30 per person, also payable to DoC.

Alternative Routes: Commercial operators based in Paihia run boat trips out to Cape Brett, and trampers can arrange to be either dropped off or picked up at the hut, subject to weather conditions. It's also possible to be dropped off or picked up at Deep Water Cove.

Information: DoC Russell, Ph 09 403 9003; Cape Brett Walkways Ltd, Ph 09 403 8823.

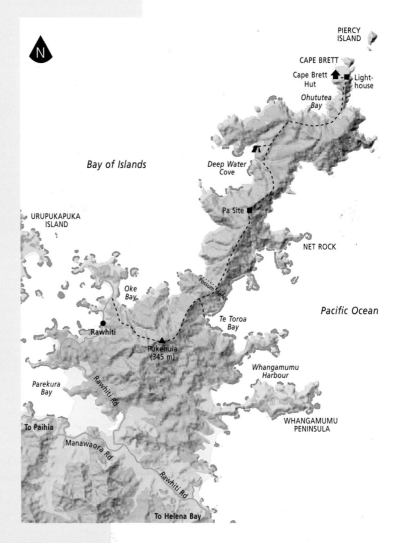

The impressive headland of Cape Brett, at the eastern boundary of the Bay of Islands, probes into the Pacific Ocean like an accusing finger. It's famed for the 'Hole in the Rock', a large natural archway in Piercy Island at the tip of the peninsula, through which boats take tourists. The cape also features a prominent lighthouse, and DoC has turned one of the former keepers' cottages into a very attractive hut. Trampers can reach this hut via the Cape Brett Walkway, which traverses the peninsula from the small coastal community of Rawhiti.

One might be fooled into thinking this is an easy coastal walk, but the rugged topography of the peninsula dictates otherwise, and reaching the hut requires a full day's walk on the sometimes testing 20-kilometre track. Note that there's very little water en route.

From Oke Bay the track leads up a series of stairs to where you get your first glimpse of the peninsula stretching away to the northeast. The track continues to climb steadily through regenerating forest typical of coastal Northland, including manuka, taraire, mahoe, silver fern, nikau palms and the occasional puriri. After crossing one small stream you reach the ridge crest at Pukehuia (345 metres) where there is a shelter and water tank. These were installed for 'Project Crimson' workers undertaking possum control in an effort to protect the stands of coastal pohutukawa at threat from browsing. Travel is generally straightforward, and the track has recently been upgraded.

From Pukehuia, the track drops to a saddle where there's often a camp used by the possum hunters. A side-track branches off towards Te Toroa Bay. Further along there are occasional viewpoints overlooking the island-studded waters of the Bay of Islands. Near the narrowest point of the peninsula you reach an electrified possum-proof fence, crossing from coast to coast. Eventually, hunters aim to eradicate possums from the peninsula tip, and this fence will ensure they don't reinvade. A gate through the fence gives access to the track beyond.

Further on, a convenient place for a break is found at a grassy knoll (288 metres), an old pa site that overlooks Net Rock to the east. From the knoll, the track ambles down to a prominent junction. The left-hand branch leads to Deep Water Cove – a

Old lighthouse, Cape Brett

30-minute side-trip to a very pleasant and sheltered bay with idyllic turquoise waters. DoC intends to build a new hut at Deepwater Cove in the near future.

Back at the track junction, continue straight on to pass into the Manawahuna/ Cape Brett Scenic Reserve. After crossing a stream, the track ascends to a commanding lookout where the cape comes into dramatic profile. Some impressive cliffs fall into the sea here, and it's rather daunting to see how far there is yet to go. Sadly, much of the extensive stands of pohutukawa that once grew here are now dead, having been decimated in the days before possum control.

Cape Brett Hut, (restored lighthouse keeper's house), Cape Brett

After sidling through forest, the track crosses quite close to Ohututea Bay before beginning a steady haul up to a grassy saddle flanked by cliffs on both sides of the peninsula. From here the last kilometre or so traverses a razorback ridge, up to a knoll, from where there are astounding views of the lighthouse, the cape and Piercy Island beyond. The final stretch is a zigzag down through buffalo grass to the hut, which is perched on a prominent flat overlooking the ocean.

Cape Brett Hut was beautifully restored in 1996 and has polished floorboards, gas cookers and 21 bunks. It's the only surviving cottage of three that once stood here to house the families of the lighthouse keepers. The old lighthouse itself was originally built in 1909 and became operational in 1910. When electrification came in the 1950s, the number of keepers was reduced to two, and then in 1978 the construction of a new automated light negated the need for any keepers at all.

Even with three families at the cape, it could be a lonely existence for both keepers and kin. The wife of one assistant keeper died in 1918, and he became so lonely that he sought a transfer from the Lighthouse Service. Then, during the 1930s, tension between families mounted to the extent that one keeper's wife suffered a breakdown.

Despite the hardships there must have been times when the keepers thanked their lucky stars for the lifestyle – perhaps during an exhilarating storm, or on a calm evening when they fished from the nearby shore. Even a brief stay in the hut gives some sense of what it must have been like to live here. On the cape's rare calm days it's possible to snorkel, and some trampers have even swum with dolphins.

For those not catching a boat back to Paihia, there is some comfort in knowing that the return plod along the walkway to Oke Bay is usually accomplished in less time as you will now be more familiar with the track.

Karekare • Whatipu

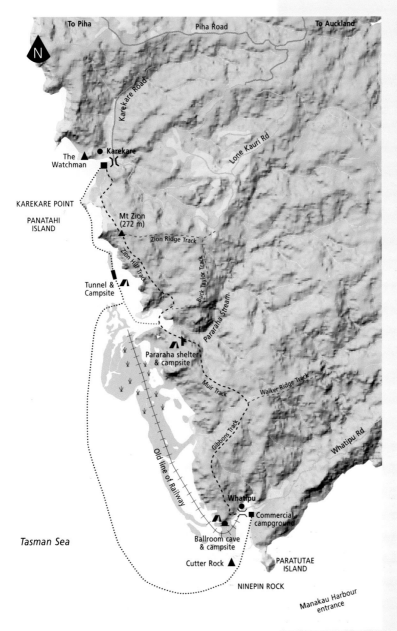

Duration: 1–2 days.

Grade: Easy–Medium.

Times: Karekare to Zion Hill Track: 20–25 minutes. Zion Hill Track to Pararaha Stream track junction: 40–60 minutes. Paraha Stream track junction to Pararaha camping area: 20 minutes. Campground to Gibbons Track: 25–30 minutes. Gibbons Track to Whatipu: 1–1.5 hours. Whatipu to Pararaha Stream via coast: 1.5–2 hours. Pararaha Stream to Karekare: 1–1.5 hours.

Map: Q11 Waitakere.

Access: From the Auckland suburb of Titirangi, follow the Scenic Drive for 10 km before turning left onto Piha Road. Follow this for 11 km, then turn left onto Karekare Road. A further 3 km takes you down to the roadend, where there is a carpark, picnic area and toilets.

Alternative routes: To shorten the trip considerably, you could simply walk as far as the Pararaha Stream, then head down to the coast and north to Karekare, thereby missing out the southern section to Whatipu.

Information: Auckland Regional Council, Ph 09 303 1530.

15

Pararaha River, Waitakere Ranges

This coastal walk is arguably one of the best overnight tramps in the Waitakere Ranges, the densely forested hills on Auckland's northwestern flank. It's a tramp through subtropical forest to a pleasant campsite beside the gorged Pararaha Stream, beyond to the ironsand and bold headlands of Whatipu, and then a coastal stroll back to Karekare. Although the trip can be completed quite comfortably in a longish day, many will want to take a tent and spread it out over a more leisurely weekend. The route lies within the Waitakere Ranges Regional Park, which is administered by the Auckland Regional Council.

The tramp begins at Karekare, a small beach community. From the carpark take the Pohutukawa Glade Walk to a picnic area. Here, a signpost indicates the start of the Zion Hill Track. A steady climb ensues up this track onto a forested spur, with some good views back over Karekare Beach and to the distinctive shape of The Watchman – a headland invariably rendered hazy by sea spray. The track is quite muddy in places, and passes through forest dominated by pohutukawa, puriri, manuka and kawakawa. After about 20–25 minutes, you'll reach Mt Zion (272 metres) and the junction where the Zion Ridge Track branches off. Stay on the Zion Hill Track. Nikau palms, rimu, tree ferns and the occasional kauri begin to make appearances, as the track traverses an undulating ridge. After crossing a small stream, you enter a kauri grove, with some sizeable trees.

The Waitakere Ranges were once covered in mature kauri forest but, not surprisingly, the demands of a growing Auckland soon meant most of it was felled. Later, farming was attempted over much of the Waitakere Ranges, but the region has since largely been left to regenerate.

The track, now increasingly rutted and muddy, crosses a second stream to join the Buck Taylor Track. Head right here, where the track drops down to a coastal wetland in the Pararaha Valley. A signpost at a track junction in the valley indicates the way to a campsite upstream. The Pararaha Stream can be sizeable in flood, and in such conditions can be difficult to cross. The walk from the junction to the campsite takes about 20 minutes. There's a shelter here amongst several grassy camping spots, with the Pararaha Stream gurgling nearby and a pyramid-shaped peak of black volcanic rock prominent beyond. The valley is lined with nikau palms, mahoe and cabbage trees, but unfortunately a growing number of weeds – including inkweed, lily, wandering willy and mist flower – pose problems on the forest floor in this warm, moist climate.

From the camp, the Muir Track climbs steadily onto a ridge, where it joins the Gibbons Track. En route, there's a good viewpoint over the mosaic of small lagoons and wetland vegetation on the beach north of Whatipu. From the viewpoint, the track descends for some distance, finally emerging at Whatipu Stream, where there is a footbridge.

As a side-trip, it's possible to follow a rough unmarked route that heads northwards before you cross the footbridge. This leads to some sea caves that were once used as shelter by Maori and, later, as a ballroom for timber workers in the 1920s. There's another campsite here, with a toilet. Beyond the caves, the track peters out. A 4WD track marked on the map is actually the line of the old Karekare–Whatipu railway, dating back to the days of timber extraction, but this passes through swampland and the coast now makes a better route to Karekare.

Nikau palm in flower, Pararaha Valley, Waitakere Ranges

Back at the footbridge over the Whatipu Stream, head towards the coast, past the commercial Whatipu campground (which is accessible by road). Beyond the campground, a track leads onto the ironsand of the beach, where you get a good vista of the wild coastline at the northern entrance of Manukau Harbour. Cutter Rock pokes up defiantly, with the impressive Paratutae Island and Ninepin Rock nearby. One of New Zealand's most famous and disastrous shipwrecks occurred here in 1863, when *HMS Orpheus* ran aground on the Manukau at the cost of 189 lives.

From Whatipu, you begin a coastal walk back to Karekare over the black sands so characteristic of Auckland's western coastline. Amazingly, as little as 100 years ago, the beach here was just a narrow strip between sea and cliffs, not the expansive two-kilometres-wide stretch of today. It's likely that this sand accumulated after being shifted from deposits on the bar.

Walking in a wild coastal environment is something of a rarity in the North Island, and this is a shoreline to savour. There's the often boisterous Tasman Sea pounding waves onto the sand, a haze of sea spray, the circling of gulls and, inland, the ever-present, brooding, forested cliffs of the Waitakere Ranges. Dotterels and oyster-catchers scurry away from you in a cartoon-like flurry of legs, and you may even decide to follow suit, shedding your boots to let the soles of your feet enjoy a sand massage.

After crossing Pararaha Stream, head inland to some large sand-dunes and join the main trail leading towards Karekare. This follows dune lands and passes another campsite at Tunnel Point, where there is an old railway engine. Large pohutukawa shade the area, and it makes a very nice spot for lunch. To the north you travel through a tunnel to emerge on the beach again, where some spectacular cliffs meet the sea. Just before Karekare Point, a narrow sidle leads around some rock platforms that can be dangerous at high tide. The notorious waves of this west coast should not be under-estimated, and at anything other than low to mid-tide you'd be best to use the high, fenced track called 'Gap Gallery' that climbs across the cliff face above the shore.

Panatahi Island lies just off the coast, and there are some interesting rock pools along the shore. At this point you'll probably be sharing the beach with fishers, families, picnickers and those out to enjoy the sea air. Once you round Karekare Point, The Watchman comes into view again, and then it's simply a short stroll inland to the carpark.

Coastline, Karekare Beach, Waitakere Ranges Regional Park

Mt Hobson/Hirakimata

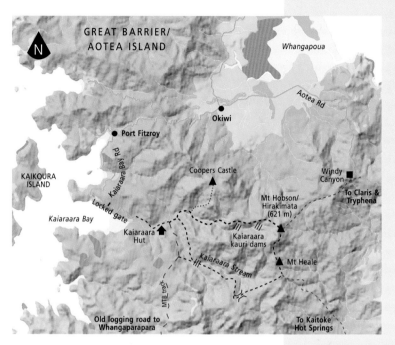

Duration: 1–2 days.

Grade: Medium.

Times: Roadend to Kaiaraara Hut (40 bunks, wood stove, Category 2): 20–30 minutes. Kaiaraara to Mt Hobson: 3–4 hours via Kaiaraara kauri dam. Mt Hobson to Kaiaraara Hut via South Fork route: 2–3 hours. Note that during heavy rain the streams flood rapidly and this can make the trip impossible.

Map: Great Barrier Island Holidaymaker Map.

Access: From Auckland you can catch a ferry to Port Fitzroy, or alternatively fly to Claris or Okiwi. For either option you'll probably need to hire a car or take a taxi to the Kaiaraara Bay Road end, which is reached from Port Fitzroy. Another option is to take a mountain bike on the ferry to Port Fitzroy, from where it's an easy ride as far as Kaiaraara Hut.

Alternative Routes: From Kaiaraara Hut, it's possible to traverse Mt Hobson and exit at Windy Canyon on the Aotea Road. Although shorter, this route requires some transport juggling.

Information: DoC Great Barrier Ph 09 429 0044, DoC Auckland Ph 09 307 9279, Great Barrier infomation Centre 09 429 0033.

Great Barrier, the largest island in the Hauraki Gulf and, indeed, the largest off the North Island's coast, is a bush-clad paradise for holidaymakers, surfers and trampers. While getting there presents a bit of a logistical exercise even for Auckland trampers, the island offers this enjoyable overnight walk with a bit of everything: a snatch of coastline, an impressive historic kauri dam, excellent birdlife, distinctive volcanic topography and some fine regenerating kauri forest. The tramp also includes the island's only hut and crosses its highest point, Mt Hobson/Hirakimata, with unsurpassed views over the Hauraki Gulf.

There's a locked gate part of the way down Kaiaraara Bay Road, restricting access beyond to those on foot or mountain bike. From here, follow the Forest Road to the Kaiaraara Stream. The track is now of 4WD width (it's an old New Zealand Forest Service logging road) and crosses Kaiaraara Stream three times before reaching Kaiaraara Hut. The hut is among tall stands of manuka and offers bunk space for 40; there are also plenty of camping spots nearby.

Just up-valley from the hut, the track forks at a signpost at the Kaiaraara Track junction. Here, take the left branch; the right follows the Forest Road to Whangapara-para (a route now popular with mountain bikers). Soon afterward, the track lapses to normal tramping width, crossing through quite lush forest that includes regenerat-

View over Port Fitzroy and Little Barrier Island from Mt Hobson

ing kauri, nikau palms and the occasional rimu. After rain, the clay soils can be quite greasy and it pays to watch your step. Head straight on at the next track junction (the right branch leads to the south fork of the Kaiaraara Stream, along which you'll return from Mt Hobson). The track climbs gradually, crossing the north fork stream a number of times, up to a signposted junction where the Coopers Castle route branches off. Take the right fork. Further along, you reach a signposted side-trip to the Kaiaraara kauri dam, one of the tramp's highlights.

The Kauri Timber Company, which also built another two dams further up-stream, constructed the Kaiaraara kauri dam in 1926. Kauri logs were skidded into the stream bed, after which all three dams would be 'tripped', combining to create a flood that swept the logs down to Kaiaraara Bay. From there, the logs were rafted to Auckland. Such was the efficiency of kauri loggers in the Kaiaraara (altogether, some 27 million metres of timber were extracted from Great Barrier Island) that operations ceased just three years later, in 1929. This lower dam is the best remaining one in New Zealand and stands as a tribute to enormous industry, destructiveness and ingenuity. DoC completed preservation work on the dam in 2000 and plan ongoing maintenance of this historic site.

Back on the main track, you sidle up-valley, crossing numerous footbridges over small watercourses. The remains of a much less impressive kauri dam are passed at one of these streams. Beyond, clear views open up through the forest of the stark volcanic cliffs on the far side of the valley, an indication that the topography is becom-ing increasingly rugged. Wooden stairs mark the start of some serious climbing, and these lead right to the summit of Mt Hobson. Shortly before the summit, you pass the signposted junction to the Kaiaraara south fork and another to Windy Canyon (an alternative way to finish the tramp).

From the trig station on top of Mt Hobson (621 metres) there are superlative views over Port Fitzroy, Kaiaraara Bay, Whangapoua Beach and Kaitoke, as well as further afield to Cuvier Island, the tip of the Coromandel Peninsula, Little Barrier Island, Hen and Chickens, Mokohinau and the Poor Knights Islands. This is undoubtedly one of the most extensive views of the Hauraki Gulf, and on a good day it's certainly a place to linger long.

After enjoying the views, take a look at the surrounding forest and several things will become apparent. First, the kauri and other trees on this summit comprise one of the few areas of virgin forest on the island. Second, the flora has an almost subalpine feel to it, with *Dracophyllum*, celery pine, *Quintinia*, mountain flax and yellow-silver pine. One reason DoC has constructed the boardwalk and stairs on the upper slopes of the mountain is to keep trampers off this fragile environment, where a number of rare plants exist; the other is to protect the burrows of black petrels (*Procellaria parkinsoni*), which nest on the summit between October and June. Some 2500 pairs nest on the island, which together with Little Barrier Island is their only remaining breeding ground.

From the summit, go back to the last track junction where a signpost indicates the way to the Kaiaraara south fork. Initially the track comprises wooden stairs, but it soon lapses into a normal tramping route – steepish, rocky and rooty. At first it passes through the mature forest that cloaks the summit, but by the time you've reached the base of the spire-shaped Mt Heale, you're in a zone of regenerating manuka, kanuka, towai and five-finger. About 30 minutes from the summit you meet the Peach Tree Track junction – bear right here, following the sign to Kaiaraara Hut.

Mature kauri forest, Mt Hobson

This track follows the stream for a short distance, then sidles along a greasy spur to reach a swingbridge. More gentle sidling across bush faces follows, until the track descends onto a spur that leads down to a fork in the South Kaiaraara Stream. Cross here and follow the track downstream to the remains of another kauri dam – this one has only a few flat boards and one main cill log remaining. By now the forest is, once again, subtropical, with nikau palms, kohekohe, puriri and taraire forming a luxuriant, handsome canopy.

Despite the destruction caused by kauri logging and burning, vigorously regenerating forest now covers the vast majority of Great Barrier. The island is also lucky enough to be devoid of both possums and mustelids. Although wild cats present a predator problem, the birdlife is extremely good, and it's an unlucky tramper who has not heard several kaka and kakariki by now.

A couple of hundred metres downstream is yet another track junction. The right fork follows the Kaiaraara south fork link to the Kaiaraara Track, while the left leads through to the Forest Road. Either way takes you back to Kaiaraara Hut.

Leitch's Clearing & Hut

Duration: 1–2 days.

Grade: Easy–Medium.

Times: Leitch's Road to Leitch's Hut (16 bunks, wood stove, Category 3) via Leitch's track: 3-4 hours.

Map: R17 Awakino.

Access: From SH3, turn off at Piopio onto Mangaotaki Road. Follow this to Mangaotaki, then turn off onto Leitch Road.

Alternative Routes: There are several other options for reaching Leitch's Hut, including starting points on the Waikawau River (7–8 hours), Gribbon Road (Mahoenui Track) 3–4 hours, Pomarangai Road 6–7 hours and Mangatoa Road 4–5 hours. All of these are medium-grade routes.

Information: DoC Te Kuiti Ph 07 878 1050.

Leitch's Hut, built by DoC in 1994, is testimony to the power of a hut in attracting people. It lies in a grassy clearing roughly at the centre of the King Country's Whareorino Forest, an area that received little attention from anyone other than the odd hunter prior to the hut's construction. A tramp into Leitch's Hut is a fairly gentle affair, suitable for families, and once there, you have the chance of seeing long-tailed bats, New Zealand falcons and bellbirds.

The track to Leitch's Hut follows an old route, intended for a road that was never built. From a signposted carpark on Leitch's Road, it climbs steadily beside a fenceline before plunging into regenerating bush. Clay soils, where exposed, can be slippery after rain, but after about an hour you reach a low, forested saddle and the boundary of Whareorino Forest. From the saddle, a well-benched trail wends its way down into the headwaters of the Awakino River, with occasional glimpses of the surrounding ridges. There are tree ferns galore, often effectively shading your view of the higher forest above, which is dominated by tawa, rata and hinau. The track finally emerges onto the northern arm of Leitch's Clearing, where there is a gate, signpost and track junction.

Head left here, following grassy flats before sidling around an attractive bend in the Awakino River. Shortly afterwards you'll come to the central part of the clearing and the spacious hut. Leitch's Hut can be popular at weekends, but for those with tents there's plenty of space to camp. From the hut's verandah views open to steep bluffs on the nearby Herangi Range, which boasts a number of subalpine plants, including bog-cushion plants and kaikawaka, neither of which are found elsewhere in the King Country. Its other distinction is the presence of native Archey's frogs, a surprise discovery in the early 1990s, as their nearest relatives live in the Coromandel, some 250 kilometres distant. Recently, these endangered frogs have become even further threatened by the *Chytrid* fungus, and DoC may close tracks in the forest to prevent its spread. During the evening, you may like to watch out for long-tailed bats flitting around, catching insects even more deftly than welcome swallows.

Surrounding macrocarpa trees provide shelter for the hut from breezes that sweep through the clearing. These trees and an eleagnus hedge (which has recently been removed) were the work of pioneer farmer Sam Leitch, who lived here for twenty years, in a whare he built himself.

Leitch's Hut at dusk, Leitch's Clearing, Awakino Valley

Leitch was one of the first surveyors to visit Whareorino, in 1902, and believing it would become valuable property he subsequently bought land around the clearing that now bears his name. It was supposed to become the hub of a busy crossroads, connecting routes from the inland towns of Mangaotaki and Mahoenui, to Waikawau on the west coast. Once Leitch had bought the land, he planted the hedge and macrocarpas, built his whare and cut bush to make the clearing. This accomplished, he drove sheep up the Awakino River to farm. Over the next twenty years the pioneer farmer toiled to extend the clearing, leading a solitary life, before becoming disillusioned when the roads never came, and finally leaving. His whare succumbed to the elements in the 1950s.

During the morning, you can make a couple of side-trips in the western and southeastern branches of the clearing and part of the way along tracks that lead to the Mangatoa and Gribbon roads respectively. Either of these can make a through trip, although both will require pre-arranged transport. Most parties return the same way they came in.

No doubt Sam Leitch would approve of the new hut, knowing that his clearing has finally become a destination, albeit for trampers, not vehicles.

Leitch's Clearing and the Awakino River

Mt Pirongia

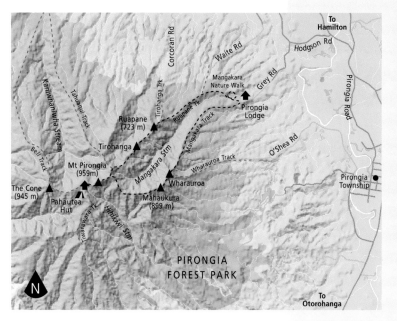

Duration: 1–2 days.

Grade: Medium.

Times: Grey Road end to Tirohanga Track: 1–1.5 hours. Tirohanga Track to Mt Pirongia summit: 2–3 hours. Summit to Pahautea Hut (six bunks, no fireplace, Category 3, formed campsites nearby): 20 minutes. Pahautea Hut to summit to Mahaukura Track to Grey Road end: 4–5 hours.

Map: S15 Te Awamutu.

Access: From Pirongia, drive north for 5 km on the Frankton–Pirongia road. Then turn left onto Bridge Road. After 1 km left onto Hodgson Road, and finally left again onto Grey Road. At the roadend, there are toilets, a carpark, an information shelter and the Pirongia Lodge.

Information: DoC Hamilton, Ph 07 838 3363.

Mt Pirongia's distinctive green summit dominates the skyline south of Hamilton. Although it no longer resembles one, the forest-clad mountain was once a large volcano. Since volcanic activity ceased some 1.5 million years ago, the erosive forces of wind, frost and water have whittled the mountain to its present shape, but from some viewpoints it is still possible to see the rough outline of where the main crater once existed.

Mt Pirongia (959 metres) is probably the most sought-after summit in the Waikato, and the views from the top alone make the effort to reach it worthwhile. The easiest access is via the Tirohanga Track, starting at Corcoran Road. However, those seeking a slightly more rugged round trip can start instead from Grey Road, taking a link track onto the Tirohanga Track and returning over the Mahaukura Track.

From the Grey Road carpark, head towards the Mangakara Nature Walk, a well-benched and gravelled track popular with families. Here, rimu and kahikatea dominate tawa, kohekohe and nikau palms. Pirongia is interesting botanically, because it marks a transition from the warmth-loving kauri forests of the north to the beech and podocarp-beech forests of the south. The park's latitude marks the naturally occurring southern limit for such species as kauri and mangeao.

After crossing the Mangakara Stream via a footbridge, turn left and follow a signposted trail that connects with the Ruapane Track. The junction with the Ruapane

Sunrise over Waikato basin from Mt Pirongia, Waikato

Track is reached shortly afterward, where you bear left (the right branch goes to Waite Road).

Some 60 to 90 minutes after leaving the carpark, you reach the main Tirohanga Track. A short, steep climb ensues to the summit of Ruapane, a rocky knoll with extensive views northward over the Waikato lowlands. From here, the track becomes narrower, climbing over or around a series of spectacular tors, some cloaked in rata and kamahi forest. The rugged nature of this ridge is better understood when you realise that it was once the lip of Pirongia's volcanic crater. The soils, too, are volcanic in origin and, as a consequence, can be very muddy after rain.

Further up, recently constructed boardwalks avoid the worst of Pirongia's once-notorious mud, and the summit is reached not long after. There's a modern viewing platform here, which you can climb to look out over the stunted forest. Panoramic views of the Waikato and of Raglan and Kawhia harbours unfold before you.

Beyond the summit, the track leads down through pahautea (a type of kaikawaka), Hall's totara and kamahi forest to Pahautea Hut. Botanically, this area is of interest not only because of the pahautea but also for the presence of the endangered root parasite *Dactylanthus taylori*.

You may see some of the latter covered in wire cages, the result of the concerted effort DoC is making to protect these plants from the ravages of possums.

For those staying overnight, the sunrise as seen from a viewpoint near the hut is superb, especially when looking down on a mist-enveloped Waikato. However, in the wrong weather Pirongia's summit can be a bleak place, and there's no water except that in the Pahautea Hut water tank, so it pays to carry your own.

In the morning, head back up to the summit and take the signposted track along the Mahaukura Track. This route is more difficult than the Tirohanga Track, but is equally rewarding and has some excellent viewpoints. There's a considerable amount of up and down involved, plus some scrambling and a few sections of steps. When its leaves are new, the spindly spiderwood, *Dracophyllum latifolium*, gives the forest a dash of red.

Mahaukura and Wharauroa are both prominent rocky knolls, offering clear views over the Waikato, the King Country and the town of Te Awamutu. At the summit of Wharauroa, a chain helps you to secure yourself around a sloping rocky section. Past the junction with the Wharauroa Route (which leads to O'Shea Road), the track passes through tawa forest at a more leisurely gradient on one of the most pleasant ridges in the park. The tramp ends back at the Grey Road carpark.

Tirohanga, Pirongia Forest Park

Pinnacles Hut

Duration: 1–2 days.

Grade: Easy–Medium.

Times: Roadend to Hydro Camp via Webb Creek: 1.5-2 hours. Hydro Camp to Pinnacles Hut (80 bunks, gas cooking rings, Category 1): 1-2 hours each way. Return climb to The Pinnacles: 1-2 hours. Hydro Camp to roadend via Billy Goat Track: 2-3 hours. Hut tickets must be booked well in advance from the visitor centre.

Map: T12 Thames.

Access: Head 2 km south of Thames on SH 25, then turn right onto the Kauaeranga Valley Road. Follow the road to its end, where there is a carpark.

Information: DoC Kauaeranga Visitor Centre, Ph 07 867 9080.

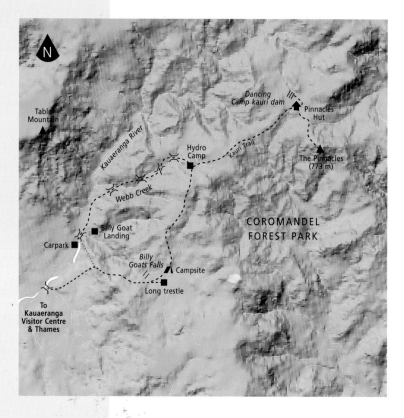

A tramp over the Kauri Trail to Pinnacles Hut offers a snapshot experience of the Coromandel Range, with its regenerating kauri forests, volcanic topography and interesting history. At 80 bunks, Pinnacles Hut is the largest in the country, and the Kauri Trail is proving an increasingly popular tramp. It begins in the Kauaeranga Valley, near Thames.

The Kauaeranga Valley remains one of Coromandel's best-known walking areas and is accessible via a winding road that ends at a series of campgrounds and picnic areas. DoC runs a excellent visitor centre 13 kilometres up the road, which gives a wealth of information on the valley's history and the surrounding conservation lands.

Between the 1870s and the 1920s the valley was a hub of activity, with a large community of people engaged in extracting kauri. From the 1870s the easier slopes were extensively felled, until in the 1890s something of a slump in the kauri industry saw a temporary halt to logging. By 1910 activity resumed, but by this time only the more inaccessible trees remained. Tramways and tracks were cut in the bush, with a hundred-odd dams constructed in the valley, often in remote places. Adjacent dams were often 'tripped' at the same time, flushing millions of metres of timber down to the flats where the logs could be hauled away. The boom of logs tumbling down in a flood of water could sometimes be heard from as far away as Thames, 18 kilometres distant. Such efficiency could not last. By 1928 virtually all of the millable kauri was gone and the valley was practically deserted.

In recent years DoC has upgraded previously existing tracks to form the Kauri Trail. From the roadend in the Kauaeranga Valley, the well-graded track crosses the Kauaeranga River via a swingbridge, then climbs through regenerating kauri forest beside Webb Creek. An enormous amount of effort has gone into upgrading this section of the track, and it is now a far cry from the muddy, rutted route that existed prior to the 1990s. En route there are some attractive falls and a few footbridges. After about two hours the track reaches the Hydro Camp, which was used as a base for workers erecting power lines over the range in the 1940s. From here, take the signposted route towards Pinnacles Hut.

The 1.5-hour trip up to the hut (built in 1995) passes through more regenerating kauri forest, eventually cresting the broad tops of the Coromandel Range. Overnight walkers can opt to camp or stay in the hut, which has solar lighting, gas cookers and a resident warden. Nearby, a short walk leads to Dancing Camp kauri dam (built in 1924), the second largest of all the kauri dams that were constructed in the valley. During 1994, DoC archaeologists partially restored the dam, using kauri logs that were washed out during an exceptionally savage flood the year before.

A popular side-trip from the hut is the steep climb up to The Pinnacles (759 metres). Be warned: this is more difficult and steeper than the rest of the trail, with ladders on some sections! However, once at the top your effort is rewarded by a superb

Pinnacles Hut, Coromandel Forest Park

panorama over the surrounding range, with the ocean visible off both sides of the Coromandel Peninsula.

From Pinnacles Hut, return to the Hydro Camp. Here, the Kauri Trail sidles along to Billy Goat Basin, past a clearing where there are basic camping facilities. Shortly beyond here, take the right-hand branch of a track junction. At one point there are good views over Billy Goat Falls – a site where many kauri logs were wastefully smashed to matchsticks over a huge drop when loggers attempted to flush them into the valley below. Beyond the falls the track drops sharply down what was called the 'Billy Goat Incline'. Here, steam haulers once lowered kauri logs safely to the valley, a later alternative to shooting them over the destructive falls.

The track reaches gentler gradients lower down and finally crosses a swingbridge over the Kauaeranga River to reach the Tarawaere carpark. The main start of the track is just 250 metres back up the road, at the Trestle View Campground.

Dancing Camp kauri dam (restored 1994), near Pinnacles Hut

Waitawheta Hut

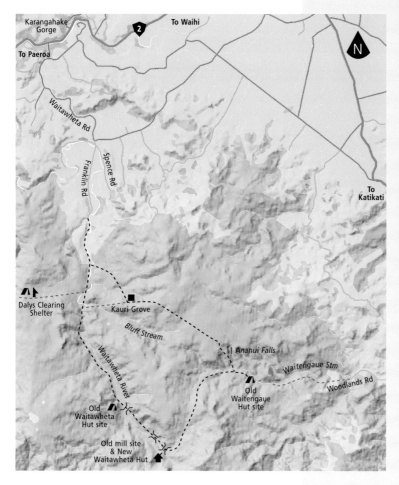

Duration: 2 days.

Grade: Easy–Medium.

Times: Franklin Road end to Waitawheta Hut (26 bunks, Category 2): 3.5–4 hours. Waitawheta Hut to Waitengaue River: 2–3 hours. Waitengaue River to Kauri Loop Track: 2–3 hours. Kauri Loop Track to Franklin Road: 1 hour.

Maps: T13 Paeroa, Kaimai-Mamuku Forest Park Map.

Access: From SH2 (which runs through the Karangahake Gorge), take Waitawheta Road, turn into Spence Road and then turn immediately into Franklin Road; there is a carpark at the roadend.

Information: DoC Tauranga, Ph 07 578 7677.

The Waitawheta River drains from the heart of the Kaimai Range, where several tracks provide opportunities for a range of weekend-length trips. Perhaps the best is a varied two-day tramp in the Waitawheta valley, which starts near the Karangahake Gorge. The route features one hut, some impressive kauri trees and an interesting history.

From Franklin Road, a good track leads up the Waitawheta valley, initially over farmland that soon merges into regenerating forest. Pass two left-hand turn-offs to the Kauri Loop Track (where you'll finish) and also a right-hand turn-off to Dalys Clearing. The track follows the route of an old tramline and subsequently progresses at a very gentle gradient. There's some particularly attractive parataniwha growing in this section, and one small waterfall.

During summer, trampers can find plenty of swimming holes for splashing around in along the sizeable Waitawheta River. You'll be getting wet regardless of the season, as there are about six major river crossings – best not attempted when the river is in high flow. At some crossings there are concrete pilings; these are the sole remains of tramway bridges that used to span the river in the kauri-logging era. The old Waitawheta Hut site, where there is ample space for camping, is passed after three to four hours.

Gorge in the Waitawheta valley, Kaimai-Mamaku Forest Park

The Waitawheta valley was first logged around 1900, a lot of the timber being used by the nearby Waihi Mining Company. Later, the Kauri Timber Company extracted kauri, floating logs downstream to the tramline, where horses pulled the timber out to Owharoa. In 1923 the tramline was extended upriver and a sawmill built. By then steam haulers and rail tractors had replaced horses. Kauri logging continued until as late as the 1940s.

Up-valley from the old hut site, a 20-minute walk leads past a viewpoint of an attractive gorge, then across the river to the new 26-bunk Waitawheta Hut. This hut is situated on an old mill site, where up to fifty men used to live during the timber industry days. Despite a few old relics, the site is mostly overgrown, although DoC plans to install some interpretation panels to explain the area's past.

Back across the river, take a track that branches off upstream to cross a low bush-covered saddle into the Waitengaue Valley. After two to three hours on this track you reach another track junction beside the Waitengaue Stream. (Note that the former Waitengaue Hut – the site of which is 15 minutes' walk downstream form the track junction – burnt down in 2002.) Unless you plan to visit the old hut site, take the track that heads northwards towards the Ananui Falls.

The track climbs steadily, until you can see the quite impressive 70-metre-high falls. Further on, after a sharp climb, you reach a signpost indicating a short side-trip to the top of the waterfall. In a setting amongst regenerating pole kauri forest, the top of the falls provides quite a giddy viewpoint down into the valley below – but take care not to get too close to the edge.

Back on the main track, you soon cross a flat saddle to join the Kauri Loop Track, some two to three hours after leaving the Waitengaue River. Here, two massive kauri trees penetrate the forest canopy; they are the largest remaining specimens in the park and were fortunately spared from logging owing to their inaccessible location. From the kauri grove it's a short walk down to the Waitawheta valley, where you ford the river and rejoin the Waitawheta Track to complete the circuit back at Franklin Road.

Kauri tree, Agathis australis

Te Rereatukahia Hut

Duration: 1–2 days.

Grade: Easy.

Times: Tuahu Track to summit: 2.5–3 hrs. Summit to Te Rereatukahia Hut (16 bunks, category 3): 1.5–2 hours. Te Rereatukahia Hut to roadend: 2 hours.

Maps: T14 Morrinsville, Kaimai-Mamaku Forest Park Map.

Access: From SH2, turn onto Hot Springs Road 5 km south of Katikati. Follow this road to the end, where there is a carpark and toilet.

Information: DoC Tauranga, Ph 07 578 7677.

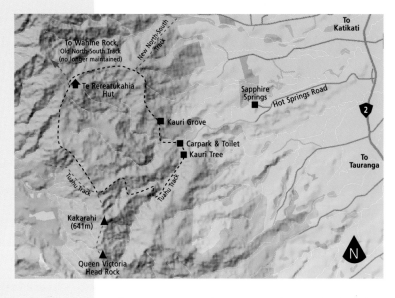

The Kaimai-Mamaku Forest Park runs the length of the Kaimai Range, a spine of mountains with similar volcanic origins to the more northerly Coromandel Range. Although there are no open tops along this walk, the crest of the range does offer good viewpoints. The circuit to Te Rereatukahia Hut can be completed easily in one day or even more leisurely over two. As well as offering good views, the track passes through some of the best remaining kauri forest in the park, here nearing its southern limit.

Even from the Hot Springs Road carpark you can see some sizeable kauri trees, emergent above the surrounding canopy. From here, take the Tuahu Track, and follow it for twenty minutes before branching off to the left on a side trail. After a five-minute stroll, this leads to a boardwalk and viewing platform around the magnificent Tuahu kauri, some 2.7 metres in diameter and with a trunk that rises 12.8 metres to its first branches.

Follow the track past the kauri tree to rejoin the Tuahu Track. Originally a Maori trail that provided access across the Kaimai Range between the Bay of Plenty and the Waikato, the Tuahu Track was reconstructed in the 1890s along a gentler gradient as required by a bridle trail. The track sidles fairly gentle slopes, crosses a stream and then climbs steadily, at one point providing views of Tauranga Harbour.

Near the summit, the vegetation becomes more stunted, and you reach a four-way track junction. Here, the main Tuahu Track continues westwards, while the North–South Track intersects it. A worthwhile side-trip is the 30-minute walk south to the knoll Kakarahi, where there are excellent viewpoints north to Mt Te Aroha and southwards across the rugged slopes of Queen Victoria Head and other craggy peaks. Westwards lie the forested summits of the Waikato's Mt Pirongia and Maungatautari.

Back at the track junction, head north. The track here can be quite muddy and in places skirts an old fenceline. While this is not a particularly interesting section, it's not too long before you reach another junction. Take the right-hand branch which, after five minutes leads to Te Rereatukahia Hut (the other branch follows the old North–South Track, which has now been re-routed past the hut).

Te Rereatukahia Hut has 16 bunks, but no wood stove or fireplace. Scrubby forest and stunted rimu trees surround the small hut clearing, where there is limited camping. As it is fairly close to the roadend, the hut gets a lot of use and can be a bit musty and dark, but it's not an unpleasant place to pass the night.

Kauri forest, near Te Rereatukahia Hut

In the morning you might be roused by the sounds of kereru, silvereyes, fantails, and grey warblers, or by the staccato call of whitehead flocks. From the hut, the track starts off a little boggy, with supplejack hanging overhead, but soon after it dries out somewhat following a gentle descent. A slight rise leads to a broad spur and a track junction. The left branch follows the new section of the re-routed North–South Track. Instead, head right, passing through an attractive stand of tall tawa trees. From a small knoll, the track drops towards Te Rereatukahia Stream, entering a large stand of pole kauri en route. While none of the trees has a diameter of more than a metre, they give a good sense of how dominant kauri once were in these forests. Several have gum oozing from their trunks, and the ground is covered with the yellow-brown spikes of jettisoned leaves.

Closer to the stream, there's a subtropical feel to the forest, with nikau palms, puriri trees, abundant ferns and occasional columns of mangemange disappearing into the canopy. A flat terrace beside the stream provides a pleasant place for a snack, then it's a hop across stepping-stones to a short uphill climb and the carpark. At the end of the trip, a relaxing soak in hot pools at the nearby Sapphire Springs campground proves well worthwhile.

Fallen kauri leaves, Kaimai-Mamaku Forest Park

Lake Waikaremoana

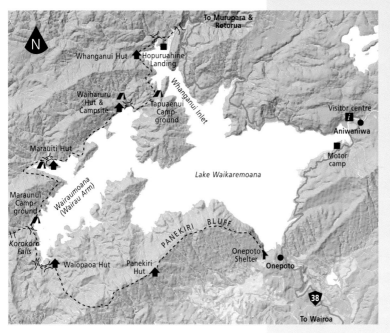

Duration: 4–5 days.

Grade: Medium.

Times: Onepoto to Panekiri Hut (36 bunks, gas heater): 4–6 hours. Panekiri to Waiopaoa Hut (21 bunks, wood stove): 3–4 hours. Waiopaoa to Marauiti Hut (26 bunks, gas heater): 4–5 hours. Marauiti to Waiharuru Hut (40 bunks, gas heater): 2 hours. Waiharuru to Whanganui Hut (18 bunks, gas heater): 2.5 hours. Whanganui to Hopuruahine roadend: 1–1.5 hours. Note: All huts are Category 1 and must be pre-booked with DoC. Respect signposted areas of private land on the lake edge through which the track passes.

Maps: W18 Waikaremoana, Te Urewera National Park Map.

Access: From SH2 at Wairoa, turn onto SH38, which leads to Lake Waikaremoana. As both ends of the tramp lie at opposite sides of the lake, you'll need to organise transport. Usually the best option is to arrange a water taxi, which departs from the motor camp. The tramp is one of the Great Walks, and huts must be booked in advance through DoC, which can also provide details about the water taxis.

Alternative Routes: Using a water taxi allows you to complete any section of the tramp rather than the whole circuit.

Information: DoC Aniwaniwa, Ph 06 837 3803.

Some of the most attractive podocarp-beech forests in the country, a large lake set in the North Island's biggest national park, and an excellent network of huts and campsites make the Lake Waikaremoana circuit a classic tramp. Although the 46-kilometre walk is a bit ambitious over the course of a normal weekend (unless you're feeling particularly energetic), it does make a good option for long weekends. These days the track is one of the nine Great Walks managed by DoC and, owing to its popularity (especially over summer and Easter), huts must be pre-hooked. While this requires some advance planning, it does ensure you have a bunk in the hut.

As the tramp only partially circumnavigates the lake, you must decide which direction to walk in. The description given below follows the clockwise direction, beginning from Onepoto on the lake's southeastern corner. The track starts a short distance up a side road, passing the Onepoto shelter en route. Although this is a Great Walk, it's far from a gravelled path and is refreshingly back country in flavour.

Initially, the track climbs steadily, but by no means steeply, through a mix of tawari, kamahi and beech. Quite quickly you gain height to emerge on top of the first viewpoint of the Panekiri Bluffs, an impressive rampart overlooking Lake Waikaremoana. The lake spreads in many directions, its long fingers probing west and north, with the forests and crumpled ridges of the northern Te Urewera beyond. There's nowhere quite like this in the park, or indeed, the whole country.

Dawn over Lake Waikaremoana from Panekiri Hut

Higher up, silver beech dominates and there are the usual forest birds: silvereyes, fantails, grey warblers and whiteheads. By the time you reach Pt 964, most of the climbing is over and the track largely follows the ridge crest, broken by regular viewpoints. Shortly before Panekiri Hut, on a sharp section of the ridge, there's a series of steps to negotiate.

Dawn at Panekiri Hut will hopefully reward you with a vista of the lake, although mist and cloud do often surround the hut and bluffs. If so, you're partially compensated by the fact that the next section of track passes through sublime silver beech forest, made even more enchanting when it's misty. Kaka and kakariki may also be heard as you pass through. The track continues to undulate along the Panekiri Range for some distance before dropping off on a spur towards the lake and Waiopaoa Hut. The current Waiopaoa Hut is set back from the lake edge, but in future years it will be replaced by a new hut to be located in a sunnier lakeside position further along the track.

From Waiopaoa Hut the track skirts the shore and changes character accordingly. The surface is more muddy and less sandy than it has been, and kanuka and wheki-ponga become dominant. These pioneer plants are reclaiming ground that was exposed after the lake level was lowered by five metres during hydro development in 1946. About an hour beyond Waiopaoa Hut you reach a side-trail that leads up to the Korokoro Falls – a diversion well worth the effort. A 20-minute stroll beside the Korokorowhaitiri Stream, which is crossed at one point, leads to the falls: an almost perfect cascade tumbling 22 metres over a straight-edged escarpment. The falls generate a fair breeze, and the viewing spot can be quite damp – a situation favoured by the kidney ferns that are prevalent there.

Back on the main track, you cross a large footbridge and pass another camping area (Korokoro), which has – like all those on the circuit – a cooking shelter complete with sinks. From the camp the track begins to sidle around some steeper parts of the lake, often through beech forest. It crosses numerous streams and there are some delightful scenes as you look through the pole beech to the soft blue water beyond. Here, you may spot kingfishers scrutinising the lake.

After the track rounds Te Kotoreotaunoa Point, it makes a long detour up a valley that drains into Maraunui Bay. This proves to be a somewhat frustrating section, as you can see your destination on the opposite bank for some time as you walk away from it.

At Maraunui there's a substantial DoC base, with the Maraunui campsite nearby. Trampers wanting a hut, however, have to cross a small peninsula to Marauiti Bay. Marauiti Hut has perhaps the nicest location of all the lakeside huts, overlooking a rounded forest headland that projects into the lake, which is often clotted with black swans.

Beyond Marauiti Hut, the track climbs over another forested peninsula, passes Te Totara and Ahimanu Bays, then crosses to an inlet at Upokororo Bay. Here lies the new Waiharuru Hut, at 40 bunks the largest of those on the Great Walk. It's set in a pleasant sunny spot, with a grassy area for camping and views of the Panekiri Range in sharp profile on the opposite side of the lake.

After departing from Waiharuru, the track leaves the Wairaumoana Inlet, the largest of those in the lake. These long arms are actually old river valleys, drowned when the lake was formed. Waikaremoana is a comparatively young lake, created some 2200 years ago when a major landslide from the nearby Ngamoko Range dammed the Waikaretaheke River. That such beauty can come from a colossal moment of destruction seems quite uplifting.

From Waiharuru Hut you cross another large footbridge, then sidle around the shore past the site of the old Te Puna Hut. From here, a significant ascent crosses over a neck of the Puketuku-tuku Peninsula. Fenn traps (for stoats) housed in wooden boxes lie beside this section of the track, part of a DoC predator control programme on the peninsula aimed at protecting the North Island brown kiwi. Kiwi are present in relatively high numbers in the forests of Te Urewera, and you're likely to hear some at night, especially if you're camping.

Misty dawn at Marauiti Bay, Lake Waikaremoana

There are some charming sections of forest here, which is a mixture of tawa and rimu with the occasional northern rata and dense areas of Smith's tree fern in the gullies. Over the other side of the peninsula you reach the final camping area,

Tapuaenui. From here the track follows the lake once again, brushing the fairly intricate shoreline of the Whanganui Inlet. Patches of kanuka intersperse with beech, and from some points you can see the road on the far side of the inlet. Depending on your mood, this is either an intrusion into your experience or a welcome sign the end is nigh!

Whanganui Hut lies at the head of the inlet and is the smallest and least used of all the huts on the Great Walk. From here, the track meanders around the shore for an hour or so, then crosses the Hopuruahine Stream via a footbridge to reach the road. If you are expecting a ride back in a water taxi, there's a landing en route.

While you might have to share the lake with boaties and increasing numbers of sea kayakers, the walk around Lake Waikaremoana really is a highlight of North Island tramping: the bold views from Panekiri contrast with the more subtle forested shore scenes, while the silent and watchful gaze of lakeside kingfishers contrasts with the harsh calls of kaka deep in the forest. All in all, this Great Walk is really a must at some point in your tramping career.

Marauiti Hut, Lake Waikaremoana

Lake Waikareiti

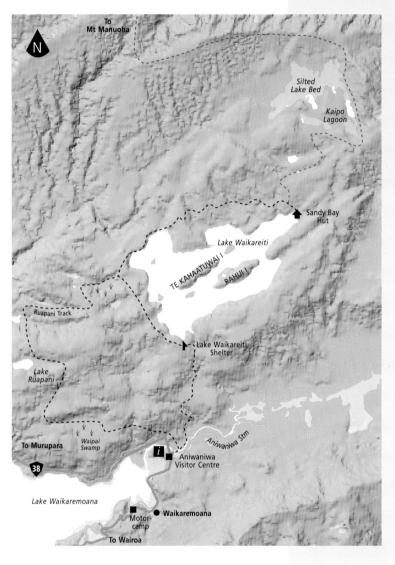

Duration: 2 days.

Grade: Easy.

Times: Aniwaniwa to Lake Waikareiti Shelter: 1 hour. Shelter to Sandy Bay Hut (18 bunks, gas heater, Category 1): 2–3 hours. (Note that the hut must be booked in advance). Return via the Ruapani Track: 5–6 hours.

Maps: W18 Waikaremoana, Te Urewera National Park Map.

Access: From SH2 at Wairoa, turn onto SH38 which leads to Lake Waikaremoana. At the small village of Waikaremoana there's a motorcamp and shop, and shortly afterwards you reach the DoC visitor centre at Aniwaniwa, which has information and toilets.

Alternative Routes: It's also possible to hire dinghies from DoC, which are stored at Lake Waikareiti Shelter. This enables you to row to Sandy Bay, exploring some of the lake's islands en route.

Information: DoC Aniwaniwa, Ph 06 837 3803.

The walk to Sandy Bay Hut on Lake Waikareiti is one of the most delightful and relaxing tramps in this book and makes an ideal destination for families. Lake Waikareiti is a small, island-studded body of water lying northeast of Lake Waikaremoana. Although both were created by large landslides, Waikareiti is a much older lake (formed some 18,000 years ago) and consequently offers gentler, subtler terrain than its larger neighbour. Tramping into Waikareiti has become increasingly popular, especially at Easter, and as a result DoC has introduced a booking system for the hut.

The track begins just a couple of hundred metres from the Aniwaniwa visitor centre and immediately plunges into dense Te Urewera forest. It's extremely well-benched and graded, climbing slowly around several broad bush faces where many of the shadier spots are lined with fuchsia. Several small streams (all bridged) are crossed before you suddenly emerge at the lake. Near the lake edge is a basic day shelter and a number of dinghies available for hire (these must be pre-booked with DoC). For those continuing on foot, the track enters the bush again, sidling away from the lake.

Lake Waikareiti, Te Urewera National Park

The Te Urewera forests here are a mixture of mainly red and silver beech combined with rimu. Unlike in many other North Island forests, the birdlife is generally abundant, and you're likely to encounter kaka, kakariki, kereru, riflemen, tomtits and robins. At night you may also hear the plaintive calls of North Island brown kiwi.

The track passes the turn-off to the Ruapani Track (an alternative return route), then sidles close to the lake edge once again at Tawari Bay. From here, nearby Te Kahaatuwai Island is clearly visible, but for now its slightly larger neighbour, Rahui Island, remains obscured. The latter is unusual in that it harbours a tiny lakelet.

From the last viewpoint the track begins to head inland quite some distance from the lake, which is not reached again until you're at Sandy Bay. Eventually, a side-track branches off to Kaipo Lagoon, signalling that you're just ten minutes from the hut.

Sandy Bay is, indeed, pleasantly sandy, making a good surface underfoot for swimming, although it's rarely warm. In winter, this can be a cold place, and it's not that unusual for snow to fall right down to the lake edge. The hut sits just back from the shore, a three-roomed affair with bunks for 18. Its verandah offers a great place from which to observe the lake during the evening – providing the sandflies are not too fierce.

A good side-trip from Sandy Bay, which takes about an hour each way, is to Kaipo

Lagoon, the remnant of a once larger lake that has slowly become silted up to form a wetland. This will eventually also be the fate of Lake Waikareiti, which is gradually becoming shallower as sediments are washed in by surrounding streams. The start of the track passes through some fine stands of red beech forest, surely the stateliest of New Zealand's four species of *Nothofagus*, and you pass some attractive wetlands containing *Dracophyllum*, *Gleichenia* ferns and sphagnum moss. Spider nursery-webs are common here, too.

For your return to Aniwaniwa from Sandy Bay, the Ruapani Track makes a good alternative, although it will take two to three hours longer. This track passes more small lakes and a couple of wetlands, which are small breaks in the otherwise extensive forest canopy. Lake Ruapani is the largest of these and is situated about halfway along the track back to Aniwaniwa. Providing botanical interest on this walk are some stands of kahikatea around the lakes and an abundance of the neinei *Dracophyllum latifolium*.

Lake Waikareiti at dawn

Mt Manuoha

Duration: 2 days.

Grade: Medium.

Times: Road to Mt Manuoha Hut (6 bunks, wood stove, Category 3): 5–6 hours.

Maps: W18 Waikaremoana, Te Urewera National Park Map.

Access: From SH2 at Wairoa, turn onto SH38, which leads to Lake Waikaremoana. After calling into the DoC visitor centre at Aniwaniwa, which has information and toilets, continue around the north-western side of the lake past the Hopuruahine Road turn-off. The start of the track to Mt Manuoha is half a kilometre further on.

Alternative Routes: For those with an extra day, the tramp to Mt Manuoha can be linked with that around Lake Waikareiti (see previous walk). From Mt Manuoha Hut to Sandy Bay Hut takes about 6–8 hours.

Information: DoC Aniwaniwa, Ph 06 837 3803.

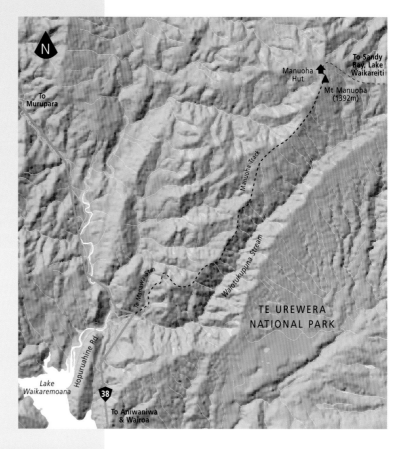

At 1392 metres, Mt Manuoha is the highest point in Te Urewera National Park and pokes just above the bushline. The top offers extensive views, and the ridge track to it passes through some of the most exquisite forest in the park. While the track is not hard, it is reasonably long and not one for those who don't enjoy forest.

From its signposted start, the track enters the forest immediately and soon crosses Te Manawa Stream. This provides the only water on the track, so it pays to fill your bottle here.

A steady climb ensues as the track ascends some steepish bush faces towards the ridge. At first, a mix of broadleaf trees including tawari combine with red and silver beech, but once you reach the ridge proper – after about an hour – silver beech begins to dominate. Although well-marked, the track can be slightly overgrown, with ferns crowding over.

The ridge is generally broad and undulating, the sort that would be a real navigational challenge without the track. Especially in light rain, travel through this forest is an almost primeval experience, the large silver beech trees heavily draped in lichens and moss, with the steady click and plop of water falling on leaves and branches. Rather than cutting a straight line, the track weaves around the larger trees. A few descents through several shallow dips are the only interruption to a slow gain in altitude, though overall you gain only 375 metres over approximately seven kilometres of ridge.

Higher up, the beech trees grow perceptibly smaller. Numerous branches lie strewn on the forest floor, testimony not only to the ridge's exposure to gales, but also a sign of how heavily weighted they are when laden with moss. With a gain in altitude, the track gets progressively muddier, corresponding to the higher rainfall. After a brief narrow section of the ridge, where there are views over some extensive slips into the Taparawera Stream, the trees become increasingly gnarled. Broadleaf, leatherwood and pink pine begin to make an appearance, and the forest grows quite dark.

Just below the summit of Manuoha, the goblin forest reaches a zenith of twistedness, with long beards of moss growing thickly over everything. Under winter snow, it looks truly fantastical. Then, for a brief moment, you break out onto the tops, where a handkerchief-sized scrap of subalpine plants grows around the summit trig station. Amongst others, the vegetation includes leather-wood, *Dracophyllum*, hebe, coprosma

Mist in silver beech forest

and mountain celery pine. On a good day there are fine views south and east of Lake Waikaremoana, and beyond to Poverty and Hawke Bays. To the west lie Mt Ruapehu and Lake Taupo, while the forested and broken expanse of Te Urewera stretches to the north.

A short distance down the other side of the mountain you plunge back into forest, where Manuoha Hut lies just five minutes from the trig. It's a small, tidy hut, although it can be damp. The following day, the return downhill trip proves significantly easier and is likely to take a couple of hours less than the ascent. Those wanting a round trip could take an extra day and use the lightly marked route that connects Manuoha with Lake Waikareiti over Pukepuke. Be aware though, that this is a very long day and the track is considerably harder.

Tramper, Mt Manuoha track

Mt Hikurangi

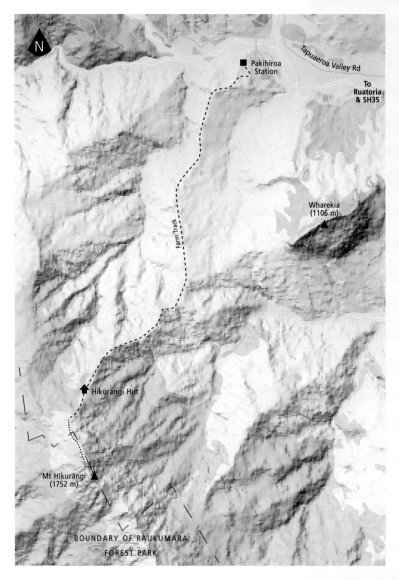

Duration: 2 days.

Grade: Medium–Hard.

Times: Roadend to Hikurangi Hut (12 bunks, wood stove, Category 3): 3.5–4 hours. Hut to summit of Mt Hikurangi: 2 hours.

Map: Y15 Hikurangi.

Access: From Gisborne, drive north along SH35 to Ruatoria. Just north of the town, turn left onto Tapuaeroa Valley Road. Follow this for some 18 km to its end at Pakihiroa Station, where there's a carpark. Permission must be sought from the Te Runanga o Ngati Porou (Ph 06 864 0962) to use the Hikurangi Hut, for which they charge a small fee. The tramp is now a gazetted walkway and access is possible all year round, except when it's closed by the iwi for lambing or for spiritual reasons. Closures are advertised in advance and can occur on a maximum of 50 days per year.

Alternative Routes: If the big climb doesn't appeal, Ngati Porou offer a guided trip onto the mountain, with 4WD access over the section of farmland.

Information: DoC Gisborne, Ph 06 869 0460.

Te Ara ki Hikurangi, the sacred mountain of east coast iwi Ngati Porou, stands as a sentinel on East Cape, overlooking what is possibly the most rugged area of the North Island – the Raukumara Range. One translation of Hikurangi (which was named after a mountain in Hawai'iki) is 'the end of the sky', and legends explain that the peak

Spaniard (speargrass) on the flanks of Mt Hikurangi

was the first place to emerge when the mythological hero Maui fished up the North Island. Hikurangi is also famous for being the first point on mainland New Zealand to see the sun.

Hikurangi's other distinguishing characteristic is less well known. At 1752 metres, it's the highest non-volcanic peak in the North Island and forms the summit of the great chain of mountains that stretches from East Cape to Wellington's Rimutaka Range.

The tramp begins at Pakihiroa Station near the head of the Tapuaeroa valley, and a long slog ensues up farmed hillsides towards the distant bush boundary and hut. The route follows a clearly marked and defined farm track, but it's a demanding and thirsty 1000 metre climb, so take plenty of water. Any farm gates you pass through should be left as you find them, and use fence stiles where they are provided. On the ascent, there are increasingly good views of the northern Raukumara Forest Park and the severely eroded hills of this part of the east coast. Eventually, at about the 1000 metre contour, the route leaves the road, and from here markers lead up a spur to the hut.

Hikurangi Hut, situated at an altitude of 1200 metres, offers commanding views and forms a convenient base from which to venture further onto Hikurangi. The Gisborne Canoe and Tramping Club built the hut in 1961, on Pakihiroa Station land that is now administered by Ngati Porou.

Beyond the hut, there is still over 500 metres of climbing to the top. Initially, there's a scramble up a steep slope behind the hut to where a marked track leads into forest. Here, you climb more gently through silver beech forest into subalpine scrub and finally emerge above the bushline. There's a tarn here, surrounded by the dead limbs of leatherwood burnt in earlier fires. Good views unfold of the rugged Rauku-mara interior, with the precipitous summits of Whanokao to the northwest – its highest peak proved so rugged that it remained unclimbed until 1946, when Colin McLeron and Adrian Primrose reached the top. Altogether it's harsh country, and off-track travel here is only for those who particularly enjoy a good thrashing.

Above the bushline, a poled route leads across tussock slopes dotted with the occasional clump of speargrass. As well as these prickly plants, the community of alpine flora includes eyebrights, North Island edelweiss, everlasting daisies and the but-tercup *Ranunculus insignis*. In botanical terms, these plants are of extra interest because many of them reach their northern limit here.

Eventually, you reach a scree gully. From here Hikurangi has the appearance of a craggy massif rather than a single peak, and as yet the summit's exact location remains unclear. Steep, loose travel leads up a gully flanked by angular precipices, until finally you emerge onto the ridge crest. The summit and trig lie a short distance to the southeast, across a somewhat exposed and narrow track. Under winter snows this ascent would be a serious undertaking, requiring some deft work with crampons and ice axe.

The views from the summit prove extensive, expanding on those already seen. One striking peak, a forested remnant lying marooned in farmland to the northeast, is the pyramid-like Wharekia. From the top you can also appreciate how far east Hikurangi lies from the main Raukumara Range, something of an anomaly for the highest peak in the area.

Whether you climb the peak in one day or overnight at the hut first, an ascent of Hikurangi is a big climb, and you cannot fail to be impressed by the ruggedness of the terrain and the aura that surrounds the place.

Tramper on Mt Hikurangi, Raukumara Forest Park

Waioeka Forest

Duration: 2–3 days.

Grade: Medium.

Times: Moanui Road to Tawa Hut (8 bunks, open fire, Category 3): 3–4 hours. Tawa Hut to Koranga Forks Hut (6 bunks, open fire, Category 3) via Kahunui Stream: 4–5 hours. Koranga Forks Hut to Moanui Road: 2.5–3 hours.

Maps: W17 Urewera, Te Urewera National Park Map.

Access: Turn off SH2, near Matawai between Gisborne and Opotiki, onto the Koranga Valley Road. Follow this for 1 km, then take the Moanui Road. Follow this for some 20 km to where DoC signs indicate the track start beside the Koranga River, near the end of the road.

Information: DoC Gisborne, 06 869 0460.

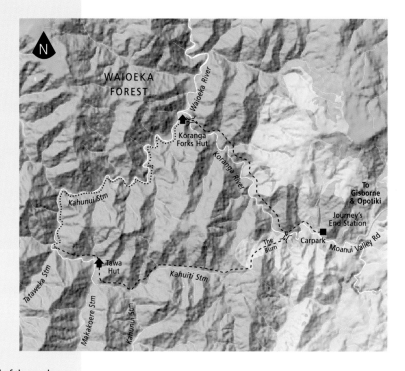

This tramp through the backblocks of Gisborne's Waioeka Forest is rarely used by anyone other than locals, but thoroughly deserves more attention.

Waioeka Forest straddles the Waioeka Gorge and lies between Te Urewera National Park to the southwest and the Raukumara Range to the north. The route incorporates two tidy huts, a beautiful river and a good chance to see blue ducks.

The tramp starts near the end of the convoluted, gravelly Moanui Road, in what must be one of Gisborne's most isolated farms, a small pocket of land hacked out of the surrounding bush. Journey's End Station marks the beginning of a two to three day trip along the Kahunui Stream and Koranga River, both tributaries of the Waioeka River.

From the DoC signpost, a track leads off through farmland and then bush on the true right of the Koranga River. After about a kilometre you reach a signposted track junction. Head left and descend briefly to where a swingbridge crosses the river. From here, you begin a climb up a poled route on a steepish farm track that the locals call, appropriately enough, 'The Burn' (it sure gets the calf muscles). This ends at a forested saddle, from where you begin a descent to the Kahuiti Stream.

The pleasant benched trail leads down through tawa forest, until the babble of the

Kahuiti Stream drowns the sound of the forest birds. About a kilometre downstream from where the Kahuiti merges with the Kahunui Stream, the track reaches Tawa Hut, a tidy six-bunk affair in a grassy clearing. There's ample camping nearby.

While this first day's stroll through the dark depths of the tawa forest comes as a cool change from other tramps in beech forest, it's the second day that will likely prove the most enjoyable. About a kilometre downstream of Tawa Hut the track ends, forcing you to take to the river. Here, deep pools swirl beside cascading rapids in a steep-sided gorge, and certainly on the map the river looks like it might require considerable swimming. It is indeed as twisted and steep-sided as the map indicates, writhing through a series of spectacularly green pools, but river crossing proves easy on gravelly sections just upstream of each set of rapids. While not to be underestimated after rain, when it quickly becomes impassable, during normal flow the river provides good travel.

In winter, the sun barely penetrates the gorge, and it can be cold going. However, like neighbouring Te Urewera National Park, the rivers here make an ideal habitat for blue ducks, and on at least one section you are quite likely to encounter some of these steel-grey birds.

The closed valley finally opens out at the junction with the Koranga River, where Koranga Forks Hut is situated. From this point, the river becomes the Waioeka and continues to gather strength until it emerges at the Waioeka Gorge on SH2.

The last day involves a scenic walk up an excellent benched track beside the Koranga River back to the Moanui Road end. Just upstream of the hut, the track initially crosses a swingbridge, then sidles along the true right of the river, passing

Blue duck, Hymenolaimus malacorhynchos

through one small section of cleared land before plunging back into bush for the final two kilometres to the roadend. When the Koranga is in high flow, you might spot the occasional party of kayakers or rafters heading downstream for the Waioeka Gorge.

While access to this tramp can be rather long and tedious, the scenery and remoteness make it well worthwhile, and as a round trip it's even more appealing.

Kahunui Stream, Waioeka Forest

Syme Hut

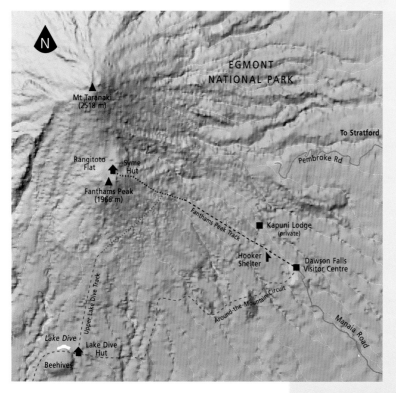

Duration: 2 days.

Grade: Medium–Hard.

Times: Dawson Falls to Hooker Shelter: 40–60 minutes. Shelter to Syme Hut (12 bunks, Category 3): 2–3 hours.

Maps: P20 Egmont, Egmont National Park Map.

Access: From Stratford on SH3, turn left onto Opunake Road, and follow this for 15 km, then turn right onto Manaia Road. This leads into the park and beyond to the Dawson Falls Visitor Centre, where there's a carpark, information, toilets and a shelter.

Alternative Routes: For a longer tramp you could return to Dawson Falls via Lake Dive.

Information: DoC Dawson Falls, Ph 025 430 248; DoC Stratford, Ph 06 765 5144.

Syme Hut is arguably the most spectacularly sited hut in the North Island and offers trampers exceptional views of Mt Taranaki and the surrounding area. It's the highest hut in Egmont National Park and lies perched on the 1962 metre Fanthams Peak (Panitahi), a subsidiary volcanic cone lying just to the south of Taranaki's main summit. While in summer this is a strenuous but straightforward tramp, during winter mountaineering skills are required.

The tramp begins at the Dawson Falls Visitor Centre, where you can get an updated weather forecast. Quite a number of short walks and track junctions exist in this area, but you can't go wrong if you follow signs saying 'summit'. The track plunges immediately into dense forest typical of Egmont National Park. Like many other North Island volcanic peaks – including Mts Tarawera, Pirongia, Karioi and Maungatautari – there's no beech forest on the mountain, and the dominant trees are instead kamahi, Hall's totara and broadleaf. In places, the moss-heavy branches of multi-stemmed kamahi interlock to give the vegetation its so-called 'goblin forest' appearance.

On the climb upward, those unfamiliar with the tracks of Egmont National Park will soon come to know one of their classic characteristics: the hundreds of steps, often just wider than your stride. These were not designed so much with the human leg in mind, but as a means of reducing the erosion of the park's notoriously fragile soils.

By the time you reach Hooker Shelter, an open three-sided affair, the forest has been reduced to subalpine scrub, mainly dominated by leatherwood. Higher up, past

the turn-off to Kapuni Lodge (a locked ski lodge belonging to the Mt Egmont Alpine Club), you reach tussock. The steps continue, climbing ever upwards. On a good day you'll soon have views over the vivid green patchwork of Taranaki farms and the startlingly sharp boundary of the park edge.

Eventually, the steps give out onto the scoria slopes of Fanthams Peak. Here, growing in compact patches, are hardy mosses, some of the highest growing plants on the mountain. Poles lead up these slopes for some distance, reaching their

Syme Hut and Mt Taranaki at dawn

steepest just below the crest of the peak. In winter, this section can be very icy and quite treacherous to those without the appropriate skills and equipment. After gaining the crest, poles sidle around to Rangitoto Flat – the expansive dip lying between Fanthams Peak and the southern slopes of Mt Taranaki itself.

Syme Hut is reached soon after. Views from here are simply sublime, particularly at dawn and dusk. Before you, looking deceptively steep, are the southern slopes of Mt Taranaki, while to the south and west is the great arc of the Taranaki Bight. Far to the east lie the forested hinterland of inland Taranaki and, on the far horizon, Mts Ruapehu and Ngauruhoe. At dawn, their far-flung summits are often suspended above an ocean of cloud, and in such conditions the sunrise from Syme Hut must surely be one of the best in the country. And at night you can watch the twinkling lights of several Taranaki towns, including Hawera, Stratford and Opunake.

Syme Hut itself has bunk space for 12, and while there's no heating it's quite cosy. The current hut (constructed in 1987/88) replaces the original Syme Hut, first built in 1929/30 by the Mt Egmont Alpine Club. The death of two climbers high on the southern slopes of Taranaki in 1928 prompted local mountain enthusiasts to form the club, and one of their first projects was to construct a shelter on Fanthams Peak. It was named after Rod Syme, one of the club's founders and an active member of the team that built the hut. Unfortunately, due to poor placement the hut frequently became buried by snow and had to be rebuilt in 1953 and again in 1970. By 1986 it was badly deformed, leaking and considered beyond repair. Materials from the old hut were kept and now form part of the entrance to an audio-visual display room in the Dawson Falls

Visitor Centre, a partial 're-creation' of the old Syme Hut.

Many people use Syme Hut as a base for climbing Taranaki, and in the right conditions this is a relatively straightforward ascent. However, the climb is not to be underestimated and should be tackled only by those with sufficient experience. Those not wanting to attempt the summit can instead spend the morning exploring the large boulders of Rangitoto Flat and Fanthams Peak itself. The peak, sometimes called a parasitic cone, was formed after lava beneath the main volcano found its way through a weak point to create a secondary vent. It was named after Fanny Fantham, who became the first European woman to climb it back in March 1887, when she was just 19.

The tramp back down to Dawson Falls naturally takes considerably less time than the ascent, although there is the option of branching off on the Lake Dive Track. This leads across the lower flanks of Fanthams Peak to Lake Dive and the Lake Dive Hut, and then back to the visitor centre on part of the lower Around-the-Mountain Circuit.

Dawn over Mts Ngauruhoe and Ruapehu from Fanthams Peak

Pouakai Range

Duration: 2 days.

Grade: Medium.

Times: North Egmont to Kaiauai Shelter: 1.5–2 hours. Kaiauai to Pouakai Hut (18 bunks, wood stove, Category 2): 2–3 hours. Pouakai to Holly Hut (18 bunks, wood stove, Category 2): 1.5–2 hours. Side-trip to Bells Falls: 30 minutes each way. Holly Hut to North Egmont: 3–4 hours.

Maps: P20 Egmont, Egmont National Park Map.

Access: From just west of Egmont Village, on SH3, turn onto Egmont Road, and follow it to the carpark at the North Egmont Visitor Centre. Here you will find information, toilets and accommodation at the historic Camphouse.

Alternative Routes: You can also reach Pouakai Hut via the Mangorei Track, which starts from Mangorei Road, south of New Plymouth. This is perhaps a better alternative in wet conditions (when the track over the Pouakai Range is very exposed), but has the disadvantage of not being a round trip.

Information: DoC North Egmont, Ph 06 756 0990; DoC Stratford, Ph 06 765 5144.

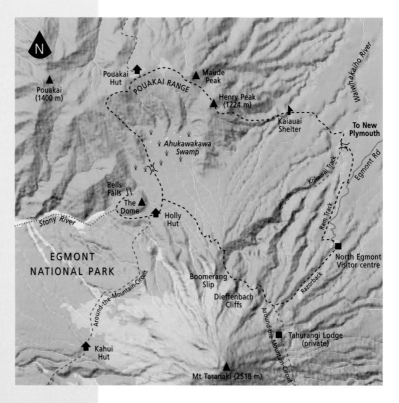

Mt Taranaki is the sort of mountain you never tire of looking at, and one of the best places to view it is from the neighbouring Pouakai Range. Lying to the north of Mt Taranaki, the range is distant enough to give vantage points not found on the flanks of the mountain itself. From here, you can enjoy looking across at Mt Taranaki, instead of the neck-straining view most often experienced on the Around-the-Mountain Circuit.

This excellent weekend tramp traverses the Pouakai Range from North Egmont, then after crossing the Ahukawakawa Swamp meets up with the northern part of the Around-the-Mountain Circuit at Holly Hut. While it's a fairly easy tramp, especially now the muddy eroded section over Henry Peak has been completely board-walked, it can be exposed in rough weather. Altogether it's a great round trip, traversing all the varieties of terrain offered in this northern part of Egmont National Park.

Several access points to the Pouakai Range are possible, but the best route begins near the North Egmont Visitor Centre, on the Ram Track. This track descends a spur above Ram Stream for about an hour, then crosses the Waiwhakaiho River on a footbridge below the confluence of the two. From here, you begin a sidle across slopes, past the old site of Kaiauai Hut (now removed and instead replaced by a nearby shelter)

and then climb up onto the Pouakai Range. At first, northern rata and podocarps dominate the forest, then you enter a band of goblin forest that becomes increasingly stunted as you gain height, with stands of the conical kaikawaka, or mountain cedar, appearing as you near the bushline. Finally, there's a chunky band of leatherwood.

As you emerge from the forest, Mt Taranaki appears quite abruptly, its stark symmetrical flanks often capped by snow. This transition from the forest onto the subalpine tops is always a sharp change in environment; a change from cluttered, cool shade to hot, open expanses – or sometimes from dripping, filtered rain to a full-on exposure to the elements.

Eyebrights and foxgloves are abundant on these tops, and beyond loom the hooded shapes of Henry and Maude on the Pouakai Range. What was until recently a slippery scramble over the gnarled knuckle of Henry Peak is now board-walked, complete with a viewing platform on top. Down the other side, fast travel down a series of woodern stairs leads to a sidle around Maude, Henry's sister peak. Shortly afterward, you reach a series of small tarns scattered on the heights of the Pouakai Range; Mt Taranaki is often reflected to fine advantage in their waters.

Mt Taranaki from Pouakai Range

There can be few places where a single mountain so dominates a landscape as the aloof and isolated Taranaki. Once, some 250,000 years ago, there was a Pouakai volcano that had a similar profile and height to Mt Taranaki. Today's Pouakai Range is a remnant of the lower slopes of that volcanic cone, whittled to its present shape by the erosive action of rivers and ice.

A short distance beyond the tarns, across boardwalks, you reach a track junction and a turn-off that leads to Pouakai Hut after five minutes. This largish hut makes a good destination for the night, with the balcony sporting a vista of New Plymouth and the northern Taranaki Bight. From nearby tops the views are even better, with the Ahukawakawa Swamp prominent in front of Mt Taranaki. This swamp formed when debris flows blocked the Stony River; today, it's a fascinating mosaic of wetland plants that have adapted to survive the acidic conditions.

The following day, you descend on a stepped track to the swamp, which is crossed on a long series of boardwalks. This landscape seems more liquid than solid – spongy, sodden and crowded with red tussock, mountain flax, sphagnum moss and a multitude of other plants. Once across, you soon intercept the Around-the-Mountain Circuit and a short distance later reach Holly Hut. Here is a chance to shed packs and make a short detour to the notable Bells Falls, where the Stony River thunders over a lava plug known as the Dome.

Back at Holly Hut, follow the Around-the-Mountain Circuit eastwards towards North Egmont. The track climbs a long series of steps then begins to sidle across a set of gorges cut by numerous streams that radiate like so many spokes from Mt Taranaki. There are some barren volcanic landscapes here, but where there's sufficient shelter foxgloves thrive, and elsewhere exposed rocks have been colonised by lichens and mosses. At about the halfway point, you pass a signposted turn-off to the Kokowai Track, an alternative route back to your car.

Boomerang Slip – named for its shape, not because it keeps recurring – is crossed without difficulty, then you pass beneath the angular columns of the Dieffenbach Cliffs. Here, the views of Taranaki become neck-straining, and somehow, this close, the mountain loses some of its grandeur and symmetry.

One final track junction is met where the high-level Around-the-Mountain Circuit branches off to the right. Instead, head left onto a descent along Razorback Ridge. From an opening on this ridge you gain your last backward glimpse of Mt Taranaki, before plunging back into forest on a knee-crunching descent to North Egmont.

Tramper crosses Ahukawakawa Swamp

Ascent Taranaki

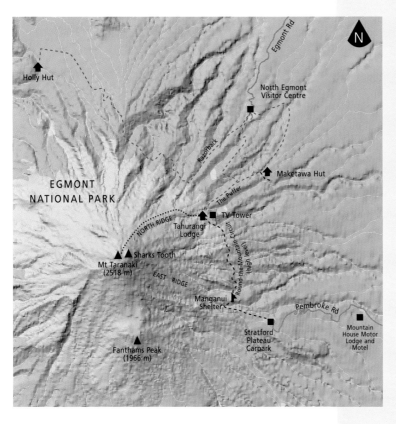

Duration: 1 day.

Grade: Hard–Mountaineering.

Times: From Stratford Plateau to Tahurangi Lodge (locked): 1.5–2 hours. Tahurangi Lodge to summit: 3–4 hours. Return from summit to Stratford Plateau: 3–4 hours.

Maps: P20 Egmont, Egmont National Park Map.

Access: From Stratford on SH3, turn onto Pembroke Road and follow this to Stratford Plateau, where there's a carpark.

Alternative Routes: You can also start from North Egmont, but while this is shorter in distance, it involves more climbing.

Information: DoC North Egmont, Ph 06 756 0990, DoC Stratford, Ph 06 765 5144.

In New Zealand, Taranaki is undoubtedly the mountain most isolated from others. Lying alone on the semi-circle of the Taranaki Bight, it commands a presence few other peaks can match, forming an irresistible attraction for climbers. An ascent of the 2518-metre-high volcano is something many trampers aspire to, but it is most emphatically not a peak to under-estimate. Over 60 people have died on its slopes – many of them ill-prepared trampers – and together with Aoraki/Mt Cook, Taranaki vies for the position of New Zealand's most lethal mountain. That said, Taranaki offers unsurpassed views, and on one of those days when fluffy coastal cloud drapes the lower slopes, an ascent leaves you seemingly suspended 'between heaven and earth'.

In the right conditions, during summer or early autumn, it's a fairly straight forward tramp up steepish scree slopes on the mountain's north side into the summit crater, then a scramble up onto the rocky summit itself. However, in winter or spring this is certainly not a tramp, but rather a mountaineering trip. Another factor to consider is Taranaki's close proximity to the sea. As the major topographical barrier in the region, the mountain literally attracts storms, and even those familiar with New Zealand's notoriously unpredictable climate can underestimate the speed with which weather changes here. Parties tackling Taranaki need to be well prepared for any weather conditions, and even during summer trampers should carry an ice axe and start early.

Stream and foxgloves, Ourisia spp, Egmont National Park

Although the most direct route starts from North Egmont, the trip described here begins from Stratford Plateau as this offers a higher altitude (1170 metres) from which to start your ascent. From the carpark on the plateau, join the upper level of the Around-the-Mountain Circuit, and head anticlockwise. Initially, the track ascends beside the deep gouge of the Manganui Gorge, site of some of the mountain's largest avalanches (it pays to seek advice about avalanche conditions before beginning your trip). Once across the gulch, the track sidles northwards, passing by the locked Manganui Ski Lodge and through some delightful alpine herbfields. During early summer, the area is alive with the blooms of the delicate Mt Egmont foxglove, which is endemic to Taranaki, and the yellow snow buttercup.

Further around, you pass the imposing prow of Warwick Castle, one of the mountain's top rock-climbing crags. Further on still, at the top of 'The Puffer' (a steep access road used to service a television transmission tower), you reach Tahurangi Lodge. This Taranaki Alpine Club hut is often locked, but if there are club members present you may be able to fill up your water bottles here. Either way, carry plenty of water, as there is still a long ascent ahead. At Tahurangi Lodge you leave the Around-the-Mountain Circuit and begin a climb up a series of wooden stairs towards the North Ridge.

These eventually give out on to steepish scoria slopes, which lead almost all the way to the summit. On a good summer's day there is usually a fair number of people heading for the top, and the route is often quite well defined. However, in poor visibility, climbers have lost their way and come to grief. There are a few poles lower down, but none higher up.

For those who are less experienced, the loose footholds in the scree take some getting used to, but upward progress comes steadily enough. This North Ridge route was the one used by the German explorer Ernst Dieffenbach in 1839. His successful climb up Taranaki with James Heberley was the first alpine ascent in New Zealand's recorded European history, although Maori had undoubtedly reached the summit during earlier centuries.

Views expand as you gain height, with New Plymouth prominent to the north and, closer, the tops of the Pouakai Range and Ahukawakawa Swamp. Ahead, the snag of the Shark's Tooth is prominent on the left, looking at this point higher than the actual summit. Aim for a prominent gap on its right. The steepest part comes just before you crest the lip of the crater, where the more solid rock of the Lizard provides surer footing. After pausing for breath and a snack on the crater rim, it's just a few minutes' scramble up rocks onto the summit. Here you're at the apex of Egmont National Park, which is scribed in a circle of surrounding forest, perfectly round save for the protrusion of the Kaitake Range. The views are astounding, and on a clear day vast tracts of the North Island are visible, and even the northern part of the South Island.

Taranaki may seem extinct, but it's really just dormant. The last eruption, in 1755, occurred less than a century before Dieffenbach's climb, and an earlier 1655 eruption destroyed the nearby fortified pa of Karaka. However, on a breathlessly calm, fine day, the summit seems to be a place of profound peace, one where you are far above the world and feel gloriously insignificant.

In summer, the descent is often an exhilarating scree run, but even the scree can become treacherous when frozen. The descent is usually the most dangerous part of any climb, and gravity awaits those moments when tiredness might relax your vigilance. If any snow lies on the summit, you'll need that ice axe, possibly crampons and, of course, the experience to use them safely.

Once back at Tahurangi Lodge, the contours become kinder on knees once again. After some 1350 metres of ascent and descent, the walk back to Stratford Plateau is likely to be accomplished with slightly less spring in your step, but you'll savour the satisfaction of having climbed the second-highest mountain in the North Island.

Climbers, Mt Taranaki

Tongariro Crossing

Duration: 1–2 days.

Grade: Medium.

Times: Roadend to Ketetahi Hut (25 bunks, gas heater, gas cooking rings): 2–3 hours. Ketetahi to Emerald Lakes: 1–2 hours. Emerald Lakes to Mangatepopo Hut (20 bunks, gas heater, gas cooking rings): 3–4 hours. Side-trip to Mt Ngauruhoe: 2.5–3 hours return. Mangatepopo Hut to roadend: 20 minutes. Note that Ketetahi and Mangatepopo are very popular Great Walk huts requiring a dated hut pass during the peak season between Labour weekend and Queens Birthday weekend. Off season both are Category 2 huts.

Maps: T19 Tongariro, Tongariro National Park Map.

Access: From Turangi, drive south on SH1 for 10 km, then turn onto SH47. The small gravel side road to the Ketetahi carpark branches off on the left after about 15 km.

Alternative Routes: The Tongariro Northern Circuit Great Walk combines the Tongariro Crossing with the Tama Lakes tramp. Very fit trampers could accomplish this in a weekend, but most would want a more leisurely 3–4 days.

Information: DoC Whakapapa, Ph 07 892 3729.

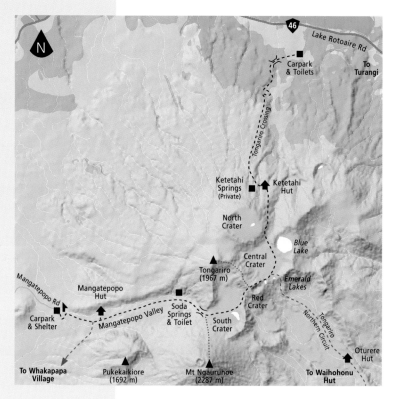

The Tongariro Crossing has in recent decades become one of the most popular tramps in the country, and it's not hard to see why. This magnificent track crosses some of the most colourful and dramatic volcanic topography anywhere on the planet, with superb views and good huts. In many ways, the crossing encapsulates the World Heritage features of Tongariro National Park in a one or two day journey. If you've a hankering for volcanic landscapes, this is definitely the tramp to do.

Be warned, however, that during summer or on fine days you will meet a steady stream of people, and it's far from a 'wilderness' experience. It's also a very exposed tramp, and one that the less experienced often underestimate. You'll need to take warm and weatherproof clothing as the weather can change from arid to arctic very quickly. And in winter, skills with an ice axe and crampons may be necessary too.

Most people walking the track in a single day start from the Mangatepopo end, but if you plan to spend a night on the track, a stay at Ketetahi Hut probably makes more sense as this will break up the length of the days better. Either way, there are transport operators based at Whakapapa, Turangi and Taupo who can drop you off and pick you up at the other end.

From the Ketetahi carpark, a well-gravelled track leads into forest and begins a gradual ascent. After crossing a stream over a footbridge, the track zigzags up a steeper section before suddenly emerging at the bushline. Ahead, steam rises from the Ketetahi Springs, dominated behind by the sharp edge of North Crater.

A gentle climb ensues through tussock landscapes, in places interrupted by introduced heather – purple when in flower – that is creeping around the park. As the slope steepens, you pass a sign marking an area of private land through which the track passes. The Ketetahi Hot Springs lie within this small parcel of land, which is owned by a local iwi, and trampers should respect their request not to visit the springs. The trail leads across some incised scoria gullies and ends with a short sidle to Ketetahi Hut. Perched with commanding views over Lake Rotoaira, Mt Pihanga, Lake Taupo and the Kaimanawa mountains, it's no wonder that Ketetahi Hut is the one of the most popular huts in the country. During peak seasons, the hut and surrounding campsites can be very busy.

Blue Lake and Mt Ngauruhoe at dawn

Above the hut, the trail begins an ascent into increasingly more barren landscapes. Zigzags lead to a long sidle into Central Crater, a large depression as desolate as a moonscape. Nearby Blue Lake offers a dazzling circle of colour in a scene otherwise dominated by earthen tones. During summer there may be a sprinkling of *Ranunculus* buttercups here, sprouting butter-yellow flowers that are in stark contrast to their surroundings.

Poles lead across the expanse of Central Crater to a scene of exquisite beauty: the aptly named Emerald Lakes, set like jewels beneath the burnt pit of Red Crater. These are three old explosion pits now filled with highly acidic water of an arresting blue-green colour that changes hue according to the light and time of day. The lakes' colour is caused by ions formed through the combination of water and minerals, mainly fumarolic sulphur.

A 'one-step-up, two-steps-down' scree climb leads up a ridge beside Red Crater to one of the outstanding viewpoints of the track. Pt 1886 is the high point of the track, both literally and figuratively. Here you can see the solid, symmetrical form of Ngauruhoe rising starkly from South Crater, with Ruapehu brooding and partially obscured behind. A side trail leads to the summit of Tongariro, at 1967 metres the lowest of the three major peaks in the park. To the north lies Pihanga, and far to the west you may be able to spot Mt Taranaki. Red Crater, an old magma dyke, steams quietly but menacingly close, its sulphur fumes lending the tramp a distinctly olfactory flavour. Altogether, it's both a visual validation for the famous Maori legend that links these peaks and an immensely creative and dynamic landscape to witness.

Once you've absorbed the power of the landscape here, a steady descent leads along a leading ridge to South Crater. After crossing this flat section of the tramp, you reach a lip overlooking the Mangatepopo valley, a place dominated by sometimes weird shapes left from previous lava flows.

From the lip, there's the option of climbing Ngauruhoe, an energy-sapping but rewarding side-trip up steepish scree slopes. Otherwise, the remainder of the tramp is downhill, with a sharp zigzag into the valley, followed by a gentle amble beside the Mangatepopo Stream.

Some of the lava sculptures here resemble strange sea creatures, while other more stubby ones seem to have the less ominous appearance of garden gnomes. Several of these lava flows, originating from Mt Ngauruhoe, have occurred over the past couple of centuries, including two in 1870, one in 1949 and at least ten during the 1954 eruptions.

Mangatepopo Hut appears on a small flat beside the stream, accessible via a two-minute side-track. Beyond, it's just 20 minutes to the Mangatepopo Road, which marks the end of one of the North Island's truly classic tramps.

Emerald Lakes during winter, Tongariro National Park

Turoa • Whakapapa

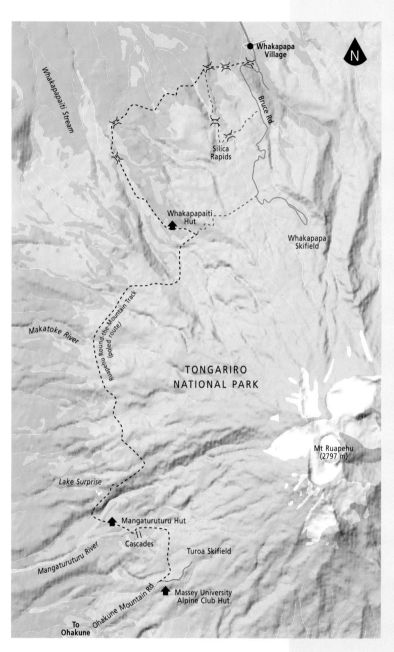

Duration: 2–3 days.

Grade: Medium.

Times: Roadend to Mangaturuturu Hut (16 bunks, wood stove, Category 2): 1–2 hours. Mangaturuturu to Whakapapaiti Hut (16 bunks, wood stove, Category 2): 5–6 hours. Whakapapaiti to Whakapapa: 2–3 hours.

Maps: S20 Ohakune, Tongariro National Park Map.

Access: From Ohakune, take the Ohakune Mountain Road which leads to Turoa Skifield. You pass the DoC Ohakune Visitor Centre a short distance out of town. The track begins above the A-frame Massey University Alpine Club Hut, at the road's 15 km mark – a point known as Wanganui Corner.

Alternative Routes: The tramp described is only part of the Ruapehu Round-the-Mountain Track, which normally takes 4–6 days.

Information: DoC Whakapapa, Ph 07 892 3729; DoC Ohakune, Ph 06 385 0010.

This tramp follows part of the Round-the-Mountain Track on the western slopes of Mt Ruapehu, between Turoa and Whakapapa. There's a mixture of tops and forest travel in this lesser-used part of the Tongariro National Park, with some fine views of Mt Ruapehu. En route are several waterfalls, one lake and two huts.

Alpine plants, Mangaturuturu Hut, Tongariro National Park

Although it is, of course, possible to walk the track in either direction, starting at the Ohakune Mountain Road means an overall descent, rather than an ascent. This also gives the advantage of a short first day, welcomed especially by those who've travelled some distance. From the road a signposted track follows poles across scoria slopes, with the bulky Ruapehu dominating the eastern horizon. Here, three peaks of the volcano (Paretetaitonga, Tahurangi and Girdlestone) are apparent, giving it an altogether different profile to those views from the south or north.

The well-defined track crosses an area of boulders from an old lava flow and soon reaches the Mangaturuturu Cascades. These are a series of cataracts rather than a single waterfall, tumbling down an unusual cream-coloured bed. The cream colour originates from silica deposited by the water, and with Ruapehu behind, the falls make a photogenic foreground. Poles lead across the stream above the falls, from where you descend sharply along the adjacent ridge.

Mangaturuturu Hut lies on the edge of a patch of mountain beech forest, just across the river from some striking lava bluffs. Such settings that combine forest, alpine plants and views are always pleasant places to spend time. The hut was built in 1958 by the Wanganui Tramping Club, which, with DoC, still maintains it. It's a somewhat unusual though cosy design, with many-paned front windows positioned to show Ruapehu to advantage.

The following day involves an exposed section of tramping that in winter or during stormy conditions could prove testing. Ruapehu's volatility should not be forgotten either – this tramp is vulnerable to lahars, large flows of volcanic ash and mud that can sweep down the mountainside at speeds of up to 50 kilometres per hour. During the 1995 eruptions, one of the 30-odd lahars that occurred destroyed a footbridge over the Whangaehu, on the southern part of the Round-the-Mountain Track. Lahars also channelled into both the Whakapapaiti and Mangaturuturu valleys.

From Mangaturuturu Hut, you first cross a branch of the Mangaturuturu River, which flows along the bed of an old lahar that swept down the valley in 1975. The river can be difficult to cross in high flow. Once across, the track begins a climb through mountain beech up a broad ridge towards Lake Surprise. Travelling in this direction, the shallow tarn of Lake Surprise won't be too startling, as you'll already have seen it from a distance the day before. On a fine, calm day it's a place to loiter, enjoying the reflections of Ruapehu on the lake surface.

Above Lake Surprise, the track climbs a series of steps before eventually emerging onto the more exposed scoria flanks of Ruapehu. The tramp sidles across these flanks for the remainder of the day, crossing numerous streams that are often incised. There are also some impressively bluffed valleys, most of them old lava flows eroded by water.

Where the elements allow, there are large areas of alpine herbfields and subalpine plants. The average elevation of the track is around 1400 metres, making it a harsh environment for both plants and trampers in bad weather, even during summer. Amongst others, the alpine plants include *Dracophyllum recurvum*, red tussock, snowberries, gentians, a buttercup and several species of daisy. One of these, the white daisy (*Celmisia incana*), is particularly prevalent, often forming large, uniform mats.

There are good views to Hauhungatahi, an old extinct volcano with partially forested flanks lying to the west. But the view that still draws your gaze most often is of the ever-dominant Ruapehu, at 2797 metres the North Island's highest peak and New Zealand's loftiest volcano. The mountain also sports the most northerly glaciers in the country and the only ones in the North Island. In summer, two of these – the Mangaturuturu and Mangaehuehu – are clearly visible from this aspect.

One of the larger rivers crossed along the tramp, and another that could prove difficult in flood, is the Whakapapaiti Stream. From the crossing point, a waterfall is clearly visible upstream, one of many that cascade over volcanic cliffs on the mountain flanks. A short distance beyond, you reach a track junction. Head left towards Whakapapaiti Hut (the right-hand branch is a possible exit route, ending at Bruce Road).

It's just 20 minutes from the junction to Whakapapaiti Hut, a large cabin set in a sheltered spot below the bushline. From here, the final day is a short one of only three hours or so, on a pleasantly untaxing section of track that largely passes through forest. A short distance down the valley from the hut, you cross the Whakapapaiti Stream and follow its true left bank for 45 minutes to the Mangahuia

Western side of the 'Round Mt Ruapehu Track'

Track turn-off. Past here, the track crosses the Whakapapaiti Stream one last time, then begins a sidle through groves of kaikawaka and cabbage trees mixed with beech forest. The last section joins the Silica Rapids Track, a high-quality day track. Sections of boardwalk across sensitive moorlands give last glimpses of Ruapehu, then there's one final stretch of forest before you emerge at Whakapapa Village.

Tama Lakes • Waihohonu

Duration: 2 days.

Grade: Medium.

Times: Roadend to Tama Saddle: 2–2.5 hours. Side-trip to Lower Tama: 20 minutes return. Side-trip Upper Tama Lake: 1.5 hours return. Tama Saddle to New Waihohonu Hut (27 bunks, gas heater, gas cooking rings, Category 1): 2.5–3 hours. New Waihohonu Hut to Desert Road: 1.5–2 hours. Note that New Waihohonu Hut is very popular and requires a dated Great Walks hut pass during the peak season between Labour weekend and Queen's Birthday weekend. Off season it's Category 2.

Maps: T19 Tongariro, T20 Ruapehu, Tongariro National Park Map.

Access: Turn off SH4 onto SH47 at National Park, southeast of Taumarunui; follow this road for 10 km. Branch off onto the signposted SH48 to Whakapapa Village. At the visitor centre here there's a carpark, toilets and information. The signposted track to Taranaki Falls starts from nearby Ngauruhoe Place.

Alternative Routes: The Tongariro Northern Circuit Great Walk combines the Tama Lakes tramp with the Tongariro Crossing. Very fit trampers could accomplish this in a weekend, but most would want a more leisurely 3–4 days.

Information: DoC Whakapapa Visitor Centre, Ph 07 892 3729.

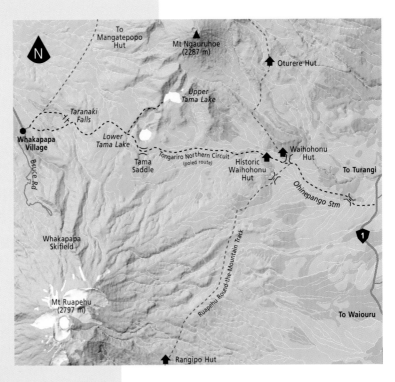

The Tama Lakes, two sizeable sky-blue alpine lakes, lie in deep craters amongst the sharply etched volcanic landscape between Mts Ngauruhoe and Ruapehu. From Whakapapa, this two-day tramp leads eastward past the Taranaki Falls to Tama Saddle, where short side trips lead to the lakes, then beyond to the New Waihohonu Hut on the eastern side of the park, and is part of the Tongariro Northern Circuit Great Walk. While crossing fairly gentle terrain, the route is very exposed to wind, snow and rain, and in poor visibility route-finding could be difficult.

From Whakapapa Village, a well-graded and gravelled track leads across alpine tussock and shrublands towards Taranaki Falls (an alternative lower route also leads to the falls, passing largely through beech forest). After about an hour you cross a footbridge over the Wairere Stream, just above

Taranaki Falls. Shortly after, a track branches off, leading down a set of stairs to the base of the falls. Here, the Wairere River plunges 20 metres over a steep escarpment created by an old lava flow. The bluff overhangs, enabling those who don't mind a dousing to creep behind the falls and enjoy an unusual perspective of them.

Back at the track junction, head east on the track leading towards Waihohonu Hut. The route follows marker poles across an increasingly barren landscape towards Tama Saddle, the low point between Ngauruhoe and Ruapehu. Both volcanoes are seen to good advantage, the classic steep-sided cone of Ngauruhoe contrasting with the more angular form of Ruapehu, here with the profile of an upturned shipwreck. In summer, this open expanse of country can be blisteringly hot, while in winter, snow often lies thickly over the area. Closer to the Tama Saddle, the volcanic soils are draped with circular clumps of the lime-green moss *Racomitrium lanuginosum*, testimony to the power of these primitive plants to cope with climatic extremes.

*Tama Lakes and Mt Ruapehu, Tongariro National Park
(Photo: Darryn Pegram/Black Robin Photography)*

An hour or two after Taranaki Falls, a signposted track branches off to the north, leading to the Upper Tama Lake. The complex topography here is a reminder that both present and past landscapes are very dynamic. Some 275,000 years ago there were probably andesitic volcanoes similar to Ngauruhoe near where the Tama Lakes lie today. The ridge systems surrounding the lakes are remnants of these volcanoes, now shaved down by erosion to their very bases.

In contrast, the explosion craters filled by both Tama Lakes are much more recent. Upper Tama Lake lies close to the base of Ngauruhoe and is the deeper and larger of the two. On a clear day, the ridge overlooking the lake makes a good spot to have some lunch and soak in the views. On such days when visibility is good, it is possible to loop back to the main track past the Lower Tama Lake.

Beyond the Tama Saddle, the high point of the track, a long and gradual descent marked by poles ensues into the Waihohonu valley. Some distance to the east, the strikingly different fault topography of the Kaimanawa Range becomes apparent.

Streams radiating from Ruapehu have carved the landscape into features that from aerial photographs resemble the slender toes of a giant creature. Even at ground level there's ample evidence of how easily water shapes such soft volcanic soils, and it's a wonder that plants survive here at all, where fragility and harshness mix in equal measure. As you lose altitude, however, the plants begin to gain a stronger hold once again. By the time subalpine shrubs appear, you've neared the end of the day's travel.

First though, is a worthwhile short visit to the historic Old Waihohonu Hut, the oldest-surviving hut in the park and, indeed, one of the oldest backcountry huts in the country. It was built in 1903/04, as a stopover for stagecoaches travelling the Desert Road between Pipiriki and Turangi. Later, the hut became a popular base for early travellers wanting to climb and ski on Ruapehu. In 1997, major restoration work was carried out on the hut, which should ensure it lasts for several decades more – providing people respect the fact that it is no longer available for overnight accommodation. Interestingly, the walls have pumice for insulation, sandwiched between double layers of iron – a fascinating example of original Kiwi backcountry architecture.

The new hut lies about 30 minutes away, down valley and across on the true left of the Waihohonu River. Like all the huts on the Tongariro Northern Circuit, it can be very popular, so be aware of this particularly during holiday periods. On a fine morning it's worth the effort to rise early and watch the dawn sun illuminate Ruapehu. Even from here, the mountain has a certain bulk to it, the sort of size that would make it still impressive if it was uplifted and deposited amongst the peaks of the Southern Alps.

For those returning to Whakapapa, it's a matter of retracing the previous day's footsteps, while for those who've made suitable travel arrangements, a shorter stroll leads out to the Desert Road. The latter track leads across more subalpine shrublands following the old Waihohonu coach road, through a section of forest and over the Ohinepango Stream via a footbridge, to end at the road.

Dawn over Mt Ruapehu and Waihohonu Valley

Bog Inn • Mt Pureora

Duration: 2 days.

Grade: Easy–Medium.

Times: Roadend to Bog Inn (4 bunks, wood stove, Category 3): 30–40 minutes. Bog Inn to Mt Pureora: 3–4 hours return.

Maps: T18 Kuratau, T17 Whakamaru.

Access: From the Western Bays Road (SH32), between Taupo and Turangi, turn onto Kakaho Road. Turn left onto Tihoi Road some 200 m past the Kakaho camping area. Mill Road branches off to the left after 7 km, then forks into Bog Inn Road after a further 1.5 km.

Alternative Routes: From the top of Mt Pureora, you can follow a marked track over to Link Road, but this will require some transport juggling.

Information: DoC Pureora, Ph 07 878 1080.

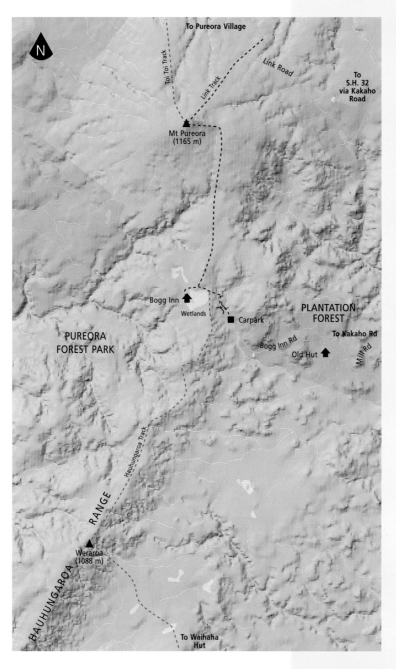

Mt Pureora is one of a series of andesitic volcanoes in the central North Island that includes the more well-known mountains of Tongariro National Park. Pureora (the highest peak in Pureora Forest Park) and its neighbour, Titiraupenga, are now both extinct but form distinctive landmarks in the country west of Lake Taupo. Although Mt Pureora is easily accessible on a day walk from Link Road near Pureora village, the tramp described here instead approaches the mountain from the south, linking it with an interesting wetland and a rustic hut called Bog Inn. Altogether, the tramp proves noteworthy for its plant diversity and for the outstanding views from Mt Pureora's summit.

Crown fern and podocarp forest, Pureora Forest Park

From the end of Bog Inn Road, the signposted track enters bush immediately, and after a ten-minute climb begins a gentle sidle around the extensive wetland where the rather insalubriously named Bog Inn is situated. Lying only half an hour from the roadend, this historic rustic hut is a cosy spot with a lot of character – it was built from Hall's totara hacked from the nearby forest. Tracks lead into the nearby bog – a striking mosaic of vegetation that includes jointed rush, various sedges, *Gleichenia* ferns and sphagnum moss. Avoid wandering past the edge of the bog, as it's a very fragile environment and, unsurprisingly, often wet.

From Bog Inn there are views of your next destination, Mt Pureora, lying to the north. Bog Inn lies at a junction with the Hauhungaroa Route, a longer 45-kilometre tramp that traverses the Hauhungaroa Range, the mountainous backbone of Pureora Forest Park. You follow part of this track to reach the summit of Mt Pureora. Although it climbs steadily, the walk is never very strenuous, and changes in the forest with the increasing altitude prove interesting. At first there's podocarp forest dominated by Hall's totara and some huge fuchsia trees, the latter with orange bark peeling off in strips.

Higher up, the vegetation changes to 'goblin forest', consisting of kamahi, *Quintinia* and more Hall's totara. The track is rutted in places and can be slippery after rain or during winter, but it's not unduly taxing. Increasingly stunted forest – now including bog pine, broadleaf and a couple of *Olearia* species – signals that the summit is near, and you soon pop out onto a scrap of subalpine herbfield (a rarity in the King Country) where there is a small clearing and a summit trig.

Although from a distance Mt Pureora (1165 metres) appears to be a flattened, rather unimpressive cone, and considerably less spectacular than neighbouring Titiraupenga, its summit does provide a superb panorama of the central North Island.

To the southeast lies the expanse of Lake Taupo, flanked by the volcanoes of Tongariro, Ngauruhoe and Ruapehu, neatly forming a line of vulcanism to remind you of Mt Pureora's origins. On a clear day you might also see Mt Taranaki far to the southwest, while surrounding you are the extensive forests of Pureora itself. The 78,000-hectare Pureora Forest Park, created in 1978, is actually larger than many of the better-known tramping parks, including the Kaweka, Kaimanawa and Whirinaki. Despite Mt Pureora's low summit, its exposed nature can make it a bleak place in bad weather, and occasional winter snowfalls are not unknown.

If you've made suitable transport arrangements, you can continue to traverse the mountain northwards on the Link Track (largely stepped and boardwalked), which leads down to Link Road (there's also another alternative track that leads down to Toi Toi Road). Otherwise, it's a plod back to Bog Inn and the walk out.

Prince of Wales fern, Leptopteris superba

Waihaha Hut

Duration: 1–2 days.

Grade: Easy.

Times: Roadend to Waihaha Hut (10 bunks, wood stove, Category 3): 3–4 hours.

Maps: T18 Kuratau.

Access: The Waihaha Track starts beside the road bridge over the Waihaha River on the Western Bays Road (SH32) between Taupo and Turangi. It's clearly signposted, and there's a carpark on the opposite side of the road.

Alternative Routes: From Waihaha Hut, it's possible to follow the Hauhungaroa Track north as far as the Mangatu River (where there's a good campsite), and then tramp down the Mangatu River to its interception with the Waihaha Track. This does, however, require good river-crossing skills and fine weather.

Information: DoC Pureora, Ph 07 878 1080.

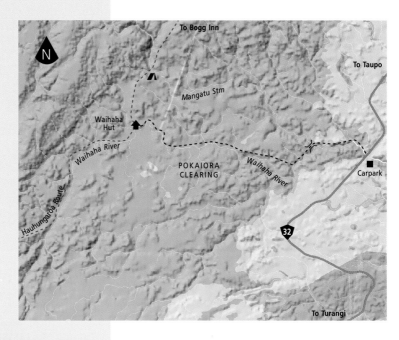

This track in the Pureora Forest Park follows the attractive Waihaha River through a succession of different forest types and ends at the new and very comfortable Waihaha Hut. Excellent birdlife is often encountered on the benched, all-weather track. As the height gain from start to finish is barely 100 metres, it makes a good destination for families or for the less physically fit.

From the Western Bays Road, the track immediately enters a section of low forest. The area is dominated by stands of golden-green celery pine (tanekaha), which lend it a brighter appearance than the more usual sombre forest tone. Initially, the track closely hugs the true left bank of the deep and slow-moving Waihaha River, with some views of outcrops of ignimbrite, a fine grained volcanic rock, on the far bank. Further up there's a brief but impressive gorge, above which the river meanders over mossy rock ledges.

There's virtually no change in gradient until you cross a footbridge over the Mangatu River, a sizeable tributary of the Waihaha. On the far side, a steady but not very steep climb ensues up onto a terrace. En route are a couple of viewpoints from where you can glimpse the edge of Lake Taupo and the central volcanoes lying to the east. The eruption of Taupo some 1800 years ago had a cataclysmic effect on Pureora, laying vast tracts of forest to waste. Although the podocarps that existed then now reign again, the composition of the forest has changed somewhat and is now largely without beech, except for a few isolated patches, one of them in the Mangatu valley.

Once you've gained the terrace, the track levels out again and soon emerges from the forest into the shrublands of the Pokiara Clearing. This fire-induced shrubland has been maintained by its openness to frosts, which have retarded invasion by forest species. There's a huge diversity of plants here, dominated by the rust-coloured monoao *Dracophyllum subulatum*. Closer inspection reveals a multitude of ferns, lichens and *Lycopodium* mosses, the latter appearing like miniature gold-coloured trees. In fact, the vegetation presents a subtle palette of varying shades, made even more colourful during the summer when many species are in flower.

By this stage you'll possibly have observed tyre marks in the soft soils of the track, a sign that mountain bikers have passed through. The track's gradient makes it suitable for mountain biking, and in recent years a ride to Waihaha Hut has become increasingly popular. Further along you get a glimpse of an impressive gorge through which the Waihaha River plunges. Aeons of erosion have carved great scalloped holes in the ignimbrite, forming a place to marvel at the artistry of water.

Not long after the gorge, the track passes into increasingly mature forest, dominated by rimu and matai above a canopy of tawa, and with large wheki-ponga in the understorey; their enormous skirts seemingly mimic those from the Victorian age. Pureora does not have such exquisitely dense stands of podocarps as those in Whirinaki, but they are impressive nonetheless, and were similarly saved from logging only after a long battle by conservationists in the 1970s. The endangered blue-wattled kokako was the symbol of that fight, and although none exists in the Waihaha

Podocarp forest, Waihaha valley, Pureora Forest Park

valley, there is a good population in the northern blocks of Pureora. Despite the absence of kokako here, you are likely to hear a heartening number of birds, including kaka, kakariki, fantails, North Island robins, tomtits, grey warblers, kereru, whitehead and tui – partially a tribute to ongoing possum control in the area.

Quite suddenly, you emerge from the dark depths of the forest into a small clearing, the edge of which is occupied by the new Waihaha Hut. This modern hut, with a spacious interior and large verandah, was opened in March 2001 after its predecessor burnt down the year before. It's a great place to enjoy the simplicity of hut life: boil the billy, cook your evening meal and perhaps retire to the verandah to listen to the evening chorus.

Along with the Bog Inn, Waihaha Hut is one of three huts linking a tramping route over the Hauhungaroa Range. If you have the time and energy, you can make a short excursion along part of this track either to the north or south. The southern route is flatter and offers chances to spy blue duck in the river.

The diversity of plant communities on the walk out more than compensates for the fact that you have to retrace your footsteps, and it also gives you another chance to hear the secretive fernbirds that live in the Pokiara Clearing.

Gorge, Waihaha River

Waipakihi Hut

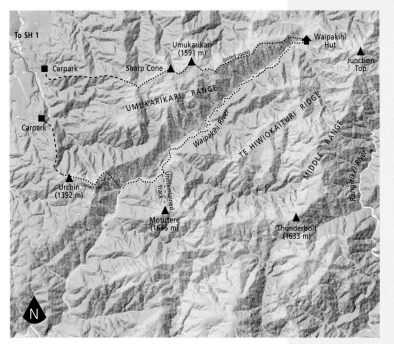

Duration: 2 days.

Grade: Medium.

Times: Roadend to Waipakihi Hut (12 bunks, wood stove, category 2) via Umukarikari Range: 4–6 hours. Waipakihi Hut via Urchin to end: 6–8 hours.

Maps: T19 Tongariro, Kaimanawa Forest Park Map.

Access: Turn left off SH1, 15 km south of Turangi onto Kaimanawa Road. After 4 km turn left onto a side road marked with a sign to the Umukarikari Track, which immediately crosses a bridge over a stream. After 500 m take a right and follow this road to the end, where there is space to park and a signpost to the track. The tramp ends on another road near by (5 km away), so you will either have to walk back to your car or arrange a lift.

Alternative routes: From Waipakihi Hut it's possible to traverse the Middle Range as far as Thunderbolt and then drop down to the river on an unmaintained route from Motutere. This would require at least an extra day, and as the route traverses some blocks of private land (in the vicinity of Junction Top) a permit must be obtained from the landowner prior to entering the area. Permits for access to these blocks are available from Air Charter Taupo, 07 378 5467.

Information: DoC Turangi, Ph 07 386 8607.

While it is undoubtedly overshadowed by the attractions of the adjacent Tongariro National Park, the Kaimanawa Range does offer some good tramping. One of the most popular overnight trips in the park is the walk over the Umukarikari Range to Waipakihi Hut. The second day involves ambling down the Waipakihi River, followed by a sharp, not-so-short climb over a peak called Urchin. Altogether this tramp makes the ideal introduction to Kaimanawa tramping and forms one of the park's few round trips that can be accomplished in a weekend.

From some viewpoints the Waipakihi valley looks like it should be in the South Island: broad tussock flats lie expansively below beech-clad spurs that rise to substantial tops.

However, chattering whiteheads on the walk in will soon dispel any illusions that you are anywhere but in the North Island. After an initially flattish walk through beech forest, the track begins a steady climb onto a

Ruapehu and Ngauruhoe from Middle Range

broad spur that you ascend for some three kilometres onto the Umukarikari Range.

While in places there are some alpine plants – noticeably tussock, *Dracophyllum recurvum*, *Celmisia spectabilis* and bluebells – the Umukarikari is typical of many broad Kaimanawa tops in that it has scant vegetation and few or no tarns. By this stage the good views westwards towards Ruapehu, Ngauruhoe and Tongariro further remind you that you are firmly in the volcanic interior of the North Island. Indeed, ash and pumice deposits from previous eruptions, particularly the massive Taupo eruption of 186 AD, are plainly obvious in Kaimanawa soils and sometimes lie several metres deep.

The Umukarikari tops prove so rolling that they almost disguise the fact you are climbing, following a poled route over Sharp Cone and onto the high point of Umukarikari (1591 metres). From here, the Waipakihi valley stretches out before you, while further east are the seemingly endless ridges of the Kaimanawa ranges and beyond, those of the Kawekas. Under heavy winter snow, the Umukarikari tops have good potential for cross-country skiing – of course, only after you have lugged your skis up! On a bleak day, however, travel along the range can be something of a slog as there's no shelter and you're exposed to weather from almost every direction.

The descent into the head of the Waipakihi River (where the hut is situated) proves as undulating as the ascent. The final section passes through subalpine scrub, crosses a small side stream and then climbs up to a bench where the 12-bunk hut lies.

This can be a popular spot on summer weekends, but if the hut is full there are plenty of spots in which to camp nearby.

Alternatively, on a hot day there are ample spots in which to camp downstream. During summer the walk down the Waipakihi River is pure delight. There are easy tussock flats for most of the way, ample swimming and, if the sun gets too much, plenty of sheltered beech enclaves where you can retire to the shade. Be warned, though, that numerous river crossings are required, and after heavy rain it would be best instead to exit back over the Umukarikari Range.

From Waipakihi Hut it takes about four to five hours to reach a signposted track leading up to Urchin (1392 metres), a tussock-covered knoll overlooking the middle reaches of the river. Nearby is a very good campsite for those who prefer to stretch the tramp over three days. The route up Urchin makes no detours: it climbs right from the start and keeps doing so until you reach the bushline some 300 vertical metres later. Your reward is excellent views over the valley.

A poled route leads for two kilometres over the tops of Urchin, then the final part of the tramp descends through beech forest to a carpark on a branch of Kaimanawa Road. The forest understorey is surprisingly lush here, with mosses, liverworts and various *Blechnum* ferns.

Waipakihi River, Kaimanawa Forest Park

Central Whirinaki Hut

Duration: 2–3 days.

Grade: Medium.

Times: Road to Mangamate Hut (9 bunks, wood stove, Category 3): 3.5–4 hours. Mangamate to Central Whirinaki Hut (25 bunks, wood stove, Category 2): 5–6 hours. Central Whirinaki Hut to road: 4–6 hours.

Map: V18 Whirinaki.

Access: Access is from State Highway 38, 18 km east of Murupara, where a signposted turn-off directs you towards the town of Minginui. Don't go into the town, but turn right across the bridge over the Whirinaki River, and then turn left onto River Road. About 1 km from the end of River Road there's a large carpark and a toilet. As vehicle break-ins can be a problem here, you may like to take advantage of the 'drop-off and pick-up' service provided by transport operators in nearby Minginui.

Alternative Routes: To shorten the trip, you could just walk to Central Whirinaki Hut and return along the same route. Some people combine this trip with a visit to the Upper Whirinaki Hut (see page 83).

Information: DoC Murupara, Ph 07 366 1080.

The track into Central Whirinaki is undoubtedly the most popular overnight tramp in Whirinaki Forest Park, and it certainly passes through some of the finest podocarp forest in the country. Superlatives often used to describe this forest include 'cathedral-like', 'dinosaur relic' and 'majestic'. The podocarp trees of Central Whirinaki certainly occur in a density rarely encountered elsewhere, and they form a unique glimpse into the type of forests that once dominated the ancient continent of Gondwana some 150 million years ago.

The track described here forms a convenient loop, combining two huts and both the Mangamate and Whirinaki valleys. From River Road, a well-benched and graded track leads through a magnificent section of forest dominated by podocarps. All five of the major podocarp species – rimu, kahikatea, miro, totara and matai – are present, and the forest really does exude a feeling of antiquity. You soon cross a footbridge over the Whirinaki, which provides a good view of the Te Whaiti Nui A Toi Canyon, an ignimbrite slot gorge through which the sizeable Whirinaki River flows swiftly.

Upstream, the track follows terraces on the true right of the river, passing the turn-off to Moerangi Hut, crossing a second footbridge and then coming to yet another fork in the track. Head left here towards Mangamate Hut. This section of track is noticeably rougher and largely follows the course of the Mangamate River with frequent river crossings. Watch out for the stinging nettle ongaonga (best avoided) and blue ducks (which will probably try to avoid you). An abundance of toetoe is a feature of many Whirinaki rivers, and the Mangamate is no exception – you'll be lucky to arrive at the hut without cuts.

Rimu trees, Central Whirinaki

Mangamate Hut was recently relocated to a sunnier and drier spot on a forested saddle at the head of Mangamate Stream. From the hut you drop briefly down into the Kakanui Stream, before surmounting another forested saddle into the Taumutu catchment. More stream travel ensues, through a magnificent stand of red beech trees, before you reach a track junction. Here, keep heading down the Taunutu Stream (unless you're planning to visit Upper Whirinaki Hut, which lies on the track heading upstream).

At the confluence of the Taumutu and Whirinaki, pass a track and footbridge leading off to the left and continue down the valley. The track is wide and well-benched once again, and the Central Whirinaki Hut is only a couple of kilometres away. This large and popular hut lacks the cosiness of the other smaller huts in the park, but you can escape any crowds by camping in one of the many spots in the surrounding flats.

Your final day, which follows a gentle track down the true right of the Whirinaki River, really is the highlight. The track's remarkably level gradient allows rapid progress, but it would be a shame to rush it, and you should allow plenty of time to admire the podocarps that often tower a neck-straining distance upwards into the canopy above.

The fact that Whirinaki can be enjoyed by trampers at all is due to the concerted and determined efforts of conservationists. Logging in the area began in 1928, and as recently as the 1970s and early 1980s the New Zealand Forest Service was still extracting timber. Lumber was then the mainstay of nearby Minginui. In the late 1970s, a group of prominent scientists – including the then Auckland University zoology professor John Morton and botany lecturer John Ogden – banded together with others in a determined effort to save the remaining forest from destruction. Morton called the forests of Whirinaki one of the most 'faithful representations of a Mesozoic plant community remaining on earth'. Their efforts finally precipitated the formation of the 55,000-hectare Whirinaki Forest Park in 1984. It was the last forest park created under the administration of the Forest Service, some three years prior to the formation of DoC.

There are many footbridges to cross en route, plus one short, five-minute side-trip to view the Whirinaki Falls. Not far beyond the falls you finally meet the Mangamate Track junction once again. The round trip now complete, it's just an amble back past the canyon and across the river to the carpark.

Mangamate Stream

Upper Whirinaki Hut

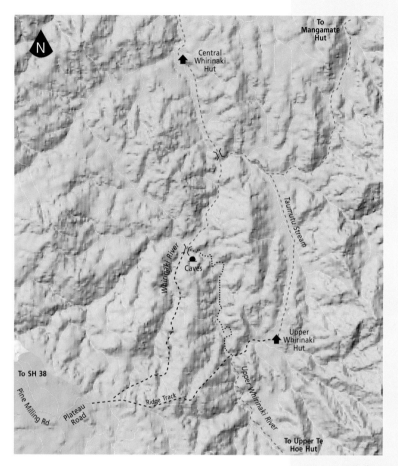

Duration: 2 days.

Grade: Easy–Medium.

Times: Plateau Road to caves: 1–2 hours. Caves to Upper Whirinaki Hut (9 bunks, wood stove, Category 3): 2 hours. Upper Whirinaki Hut to Plateau Road via ridge track: 2.5–3 hours.

Map: V18 Whirinaki.

Access: Access to Plateau Road, where the track starts, is through Kaingaroa Forest off SH38 near Murupara. Make sure you have a good map for negotiating the potentially confusing myriad of logging roads to get there. Normally there are no access restrictions, but during periods of logging or high fire risk it may be a good idea to check with Fletcher Challenge before your trip (Ph 07 366 1000).

Alternative routes: Some people combine a visit to Upper Whirinaki Hut with the tramp into Central Whirinaki (see page 80).

Information: DoC Murupara, Ph 07 366 1080.

This is a lesser-known but pleasant two-day tramp to Upper Whirinaki Hut, which lies in the southwestern corner of Whirinaki Forest Park. It's a fairly easy round trip, with undulating bush tracks, no major climbs and one section of river travel. Although it lacks the 'cathedral-like' podocarp groves of Central Whirinaki, the tramp is usually quieter and there are good opportunities to see blue duck in the river section.

From the carpark at the end of Plateau Road, a well-benched track winds its way around the spurs of a bush ridge towards the Whirinaki River. Beech forest dominates here, with occasional podocarps – mainly rimu – breaking the uniformity of the canopy. Large mountain cabbage trees, or ti toi, frequently hang like umbrellas over the track. After a couple of hours you reach the main Whirinaki River at a footbridge. Nearby caves marked on the map are accessible as a short side-trip from here, and the larger one harbours glow-worms. These are not true limestone caves but were formed as the stream excavated the highly erodable pumice deposits.

Once across the footbridge, you come to a track junction; head upstream (the other track leads to Central Whirinaki). The track now meanders, crossing the river in places that are mostly shallow and easily forded. There's nothing strenuous about travel up this attractive upper section of the Whirinaki River, but when it is in flood the trip would prove impossible. This easy tramping leaves plenty of energy to listen out for the kaka and kakariki, which are still relatively abundant in the area, or perhaps for contemplation of the surrounding topography.

Whirinaki is essentially a heavily dissected landscape lying between the plains of the Kaingaroa to the west and the fault mountains of the Te Urewera National Park to the east. Covering the underlying ignimbrite and greywacke are layers of ash and pumice, and the latter is often seen in the river. During the 1995/96 Ruapehu eruptions, much of Whirinaki's forests were covered in a fine layer of ash. While the power of the volcano to emit ash over such distances is astonishing, these latest Ruapehu rumbles were but minor episodes in the area's long history of vulcanism. When Taupo last erupted around 186 AD, the Chinese noted the explosion, and it remains the largest eruption in the world's recorded history. This catastrophic event significantly affected the topography and vegetation of surrounding areas such as Whirinaki.

About two kilometres upstream of the swingbridge, you reach a prominent sign-posted four-way track junction. To the south, the track continues up-valley and

Whirinaki River, Whirinaki Forest Park

eventually passes into the Te Hoe catchment. To the west lies your route out over a bush ridge back to Plateau Road, while to the east lies Upper Whirinaki Hut, now just a 20-minute amble away up a small tributary of the main river. The hut, tidy like all of those in the park, is situated at the far end of a grassy clearing with a prominent podocarp rising on the left. In recent years it has been upgraded and now has nine bunks and a wood stove – perfect for cold winter weekends.

On the final day, trace your route back to the track junction. Take the signposted track leading to Plateau Road, which climbs briskly up onto a bush ridge. While this is a rougher trail than the well-maintained and benched track of the first leg of the tramp, it offers a good way to complete the round trip.

Crown fern and red beech trees

Arahaki Lagoon

Duration: 1 day.

Grade: Easy.

Times: Road to Arahaki Lagoon: 2–3 hours return.

Map: V18 Whirinaki.

Access: Access is from SH38, 18 km east of Murupara, where a signposted turn-off directs you towards the town of Minginui. Don't go into the town, but turn right across the bridge over the Whirinaki River, and then turn left onto River Road. The track to Arahaki Lagoon branches off at the roadend.

Information: DoC Murupara, Ph 07 366 1080.

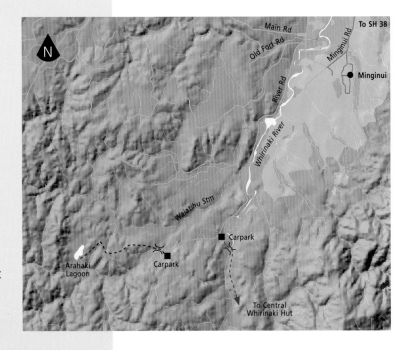

Arahaki Lagoon, surrounded by a solid wall of dense kahikatea forest (New Zealand's tallest and perhaps most elegant tree), is undoubtedly one of the most magnificent wetlands in the country. This track into the lagoon is well-graded and benched, making it suitable for families and those who are less physically fit, and can be accomplished in just half a day. While Arahaki Lagoon is not suitable for an overnight tramp, there is a camping area near Minginui, or it can be combined with a visit to Central Whirinaki.

From the roadend, the track soon leads onto a footbridge over the Waiatiu Stream, then begins a gentle sidle onto a flattish bush terrace. The track has recently been widened and re-routed, passing through fine podocarp/hardwood forest, with mature matai and miro the most noticeable emergent trees. In some places there are stands of tawa, an attractive tree whose dense foliage shades the forest floor to a degree achieved by few others. In other places, thick groves of Smith's tree-fern line the trailside.

After 60–90 minutes, depending on your pace, you reach a small arm of the lagoon where the track ends. Here, surrounding the lagoon, is the largest stand of kahikatea forest in Whirinaki Forest Park. Undoubtedly the lagoon appears at its most striking after heavy rain, when the water laps into the surrounding forest. Under such conditions, the fantastically buttressed and moss-encrusted kahikatea trees rise arrow-straight out of the lagoon edge, forming one of the most exquisite scenes in the North

Island. In calm conditions the reflections, if anything, exacerbate the apparent height of the trees, which can reach up to 60 metres.

After dry periods, the aquatic foliage (largely sedges) and lower buttresses of the kahikatea trees are exposed, and without the same level of reflection the lagoon's beauty is more subdued. However, under such conditions you are able to examine more closely the myriad plants growing on the kahikatea trunks, including the attractive hanging spleenwort and wispy *Usnea* lichens. You may also hear the chirrup of frogs here; these are not native amphibians, but one of three Australian species that have adapted well to New Zealand. Towards evening, long-tailed bats might be seen flitting around the forest edge.

While there are no tracks around it, the lagoon edge is a place to dally, have some lunch and appreciate one of Whirinaki's rare sights – a place open enough to allow you to see the wood for the trees.

Cyathea smithii – *tree fern*
OVERLEAF: Kahikatea trees, Arahaki Lagoon, Whirinaki Forest Park

Te Puia Lodge

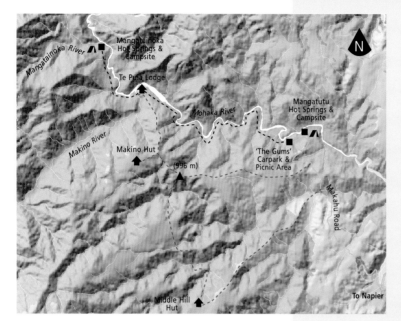

Duration: 2 days.

Grade: Easy.

Times: Makahu Road to Te Puia Lodge (24 bunks, gas heater and cooking rings, Category 2): 2.5–3 hours. Te Puia to Mangatainoka Hot Springs: 30–40 minutes each way.

Maps: U20 Kaweka, U19 Kaimanawa, Kaweka Forest Park Map.

Access: From Napier, it's a 60-km drive to Puketitiri. Shortly afterwards, the road forks; turn right here into Hot Springs Road. Follow this for 6 km, then turn left onto Makahu Road and continue to the end.

Alternative: From Te Puia Lodge, it's possible to complete a round trip back to the car via Makino Hut. This is longer and involves quite a climb.

Information: DoC Napier, Ph 06 834 3111; DoC Puketitiri, Ph 06 839 8882.

A large hut, a sizeable river with good swimming holes and hot pools at both the start and end of the tramp – what more could you ask for? This easy tramp in Kaweka Forest Park was made for a luxurious weekend, and the hot springs are a real treat, especially during the winter. From the Mangatutu Hot Springs, the track follows the Mohaka River to Te Puia Lodge, where a short diversion is possible up to the Mangatainoka Hot Springs.

'The Gums', a carpark and camping area at the end of Makahu Road, is reached only after a long and very windy drive inland from Napier. Once there, however, you do not need to shoulder your pack immediately. Some 500 metres back along the road, a five-minute walk leads to the well-developed Mangatutu Hot Springs, where an old fisheries tub is partially sunk into a wooden deck. There's room for four to five people, and a dip makes a very pleasant way to begin your tramp (note: keep your head above water to prevent any chance of contracting amoebic meningitis).

Local Maori were well familiar with the Mangatutu Hot Springs and had settlements near here and at the Mangatainoka Hot Springs, where they caught eels in the Mohaka. The first Pakeha route, suitable for horse-drawn vehicles, came through in 1915 but soon deteriorated. Then, in 1962, the New Zealand Forest Service opened a road, although it was not until 1990 that access became possible by two-wheel drive.

Mohaka River, Kaweka Forest Park

Beware of soaking too long, or you'll reach such a state of torpor that even the two or three-hour walk to Te Puia Lodge will seem just too much. From the carpark, the track climbs up and down for a short section before crossing a small creek and heading north onto some open flats beside the Mohaka River. The Mohaka is one of the principal rivers of the Kaweka Range and is a large body of water well-known for its good trout fishing and excellent rafting. The vegetation here is mostly regenerating following burning of the primary forest by early graziers and is at first dominated by kanuka and manuka. Both trees are eye-catching when in flower, when they sometimes give the appearance of being covered by a light sprinkling of snow.

After rounding a shoulder, the track heads westward again and along to a pleasant gravelly beach, where there is a large swimming hole and some river reflections. The next section of track has literally been carved out of the cliffside, a result of improvements made during the 1960s when there was a proposal to develop a high-grade east–west track across the Kawekas. Considering the rather precipitous nature of the Mohaka Valley, the track is generally easy, although there are four high sidles above the river to avoid bluffs. About 40 minutes from the hut, the river takes a striking 'S' bend, with an impressive cliff on the far bank. The track zigzags steeply onto a shoulder with a view of a straight section of the river, here featuring an island. There is much more mature beech forest now, particularly on the true left. From here to the hut the track remains fairly level.

Although it has bunk space for 24, Te Puia Lodge is popular with school groups and families and so can get quite full during weekends. It lies on an open flat beside a beach and rapid in the Mohaka. After settling into the hut and enjoying a cup of tea, most visitors choose to wander up-river to the Mangatainoka Hot Springs for an evening soak. After crossing the Makino River on a swingbridge, the track sidles around the Mohaka to a steepish clamber up a narrow spur. This leads onto a flat terrace and finally down to the river flats again. Here, surrounding a good camping area, are some fine podocarps – including rimu, matai and kahikatea – with the hot springs nearby. Surrounded by a deck are two fibreglass tubs, which are filled with an adjustable pipe fed by hot water issuing from a bank. If the pools are cold on arrival, you may need to wait 30 minutes or so before the water reaches a suitably languorous temperature. The upper tub overflows into the lower one, and some scoops provide a means of adjusting the temperature in each. Taking a soak is a great way to relax during the evening, perhaps sipping some wine as you listen to the moreporks or even – if you're lucky – a North Island brown kiwi.

If the moon is not out, you'll need torches for the stroll back to Te Puia Lodge. The following day, it's simply a matter of walking back out. Alternatively, if you prefer a longer round trip, you can climb up to Makino Hut and reach the road by a connecting bush track. Either way, back at the carpark you may as well have one last soak in the Mangatutu Hot Springs.

Trampers in Mangatainoka hot pools

Ascent Kaweka J

KAWEKA FOREST PARK, HAWKES BAY

Duration: 1–2 days.

Grade: Medium.

Times: Makahu Saddle to Dominie Biv (2 bunks, Category 4): 1.5–2 hours. Dominie to Kaweka J: 1–1.5 hours. Kaweka J to Back Ridge Hut (4 bunks, wood stove, Category 3): 2–3 hours.

Maps: U20 Kaweka, Kaweka Forest Park Map.

Access: From Napier, it's a 60-km drive to Puketitiri. Shortly afterwards, the road forks; turn left here into Whittle Road and follow this for 5 km until you reach another road junction. Turn right onto Kaweka Road and follow this past Little Clearing to Makahu Saddle, where there are toilets, carpark and a 4-bunk hut. In winter, heavy snowfalls on Kaweka can make chains necessary.

Alternative: Those who prefer a daytrip can simply climb to Kaweka J and return. Those wanting a slightly longer overnight trip can go on to climb North Kaweka from Back Ridge Hut, then descend eastwards on Pinnacles Spur to intercept the Kaweka Flats Track, which is followed back to Makahu Saddle.

Information: DoC Napier, Ph 06 834 3111; DoC Puketitiri, Ph 06 839 8882.

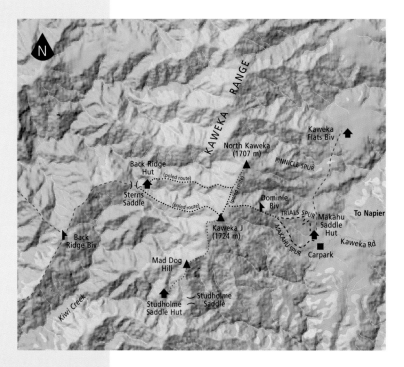

Kaweka J is the highest peak in the Kaweka Range at 1724 metres, and the fourth-highest non-volcanic peak in the North Island after Hikurangi, Mangaweka and Makorako. It's an accessible and popular summit that is reached from Makahu Saddle, a high plateau lying to the east, and as the start point lies at the lofty altitude of 970 metres, the ascent is not as demanding as for those peaks mentioned above. From the top there are views across the North Island stretching from the Pacific Ocean and Hawke Bay in the east, to the volcanic plateau in the west. There's a biv en route and a hut at the end of the day.

From Makahu Saddle, the Kaweka Range rises abruptly in front of you, several semi-forested spurs joining the ridge crest like ribs to a backbone. This severely eroded part of the range has suffered heavily under human influence, with a chequered history of fires, sheep grazing, damage by deer and disastrous revegetation programmes that used lodgepole pine (*Pinus contorta*), which unfortunately later proved to be an aggressive weed. Under the glaring and revealing light of a summer sun the area does not have an attractive outlook by any means, but under a mantle of winter snow it can assume the appearance of a softer and more likeable landscape.

Despite its scenic shortcomings, the 750-metre climb to Kaweka J is not without reward. From the carpark, a signposted track leads past Makahu Saddle Hut then begins a zigzag ascent of Trials Spur. During summer there is scant water on these tops, and you'll need to carry plenty with you. The track used to push through lodgepole pine, but in a concerted effort DoC has recently felled all those in the area. You soon reach the subalpine herbfields, where Trials Spur joins the upper Makahu Spur. Ten minutes from here is Dominie Biv, perched on a flat shoulder with commanding views of North Kaweka. There's a water tank at the biv, which makes it a convenient spot to have some lunch or peruse the hut book.

Above the biv, the climb continues along a well-travelled route that is both poled and clearly defined. It sidles around a few rocky outcrops, then the gradient begins to ease off near the crest of the range. On top, you intercept a poled route. Head south, where a flat section of tops leads ever so slightly upwards to Kaweka J. Apart from a battered trig and a large cairn here (originally built by the Heretaunga Tramping Club as a memorial to members lost in World War II, and added to by generations of trampers ever since), you could be forgiven for not knowing this is the summit of the Kawekas, so undulating is the terrain. There are extensive views in every direction, with the rumpled, forested ridges of the Kawekas and Kaimanawas finally giving way to the more desolate terrain of the central volcanoes on the western horizon.

The Kawekas receive less rainfall than areas further west or north, and at first the tops here appear a little barren. But closer inspection reveals quite a diversity of alpine

Dawn over Makahu Spur, Kaweka Forest Park

plants, ranging from bluebells to the prostrate and curved-leaf *Dracophyllum recurvum*, two species of mountain daisy, rock cushion, a speargrass, a bristly carrot and the buttercup korikori. These plants mostly grow in the slight shelter provided by small scree hummocks, where they can partly escape the desiccating wind. In winter, the Kaweka Range can get heavy dumps of snow, particularly from easterly storms, and the plants have different pressures to cope with. Trampers, too, should note that the tops can be treacherous in bad weather, as they are exposed to winds from every direction.

Back Ridge Hut

After adding a couple of rocks to the cairn, head off down towards a poled route that leads to Back Ridge Hut. In misty conditions you'll need to pay sharp attention to your map, and compass work may be essential to find the correct spur. There are two spurs that lead westward to Back Ridge Hut: one that branches off very near Kaweka J and another that does so about a kilometre to the north. Take the more southerly spur, which descends gently and gets better defined as you go. Once you reach the bush edge, it's a short distance to Sterns Saddle, where a track branches off steeply to Back Ridge Hut. This lies in an attractive hollow beside a patch of mountain beech forest with a babbling brook nearby.

Back Ridge Hut is one of only two deer culler huts constructed using Dexion aluminium framing (the other being Makahu Saddle Hut). The New Zealand Forest Service built it in 1957 with materials air-dropped from a plane. Later huts could be built using timber frames, as by then helicopters enabled these more bulky materials to be transported into the back country. The hut is painted a traditional Forest Service orange, and along with its surrounds, it seems to embody the Kaweka experience. So many of the huts in the park – including Tira Lodge, Ballard, Studholme Saddle, Kiwi Saddle, Mangaturutu, Manson and Back Ridge Biv – occupy sites just on the bush edge, often in small, attractive clearings whose edges are lapped by subalpine plants. It's a subtle sort of beauty, lacking the sharp peaks of the Ruahines or the bold summits of the Tararuas, but with appeal nonetheless.

The following day, follow the track that climbs steeply onto a spur to the north of the hut, then ascend at a more leisurely pace back to the crest of the Kaweka Range. This spur is liberally poled, and you shouldn't have any navigation problems as long as you keep going uphill. Once back on the poled route leading across the main range, it seems a shame not to make an excursion to North Kaweka (1707 metres) now you're so close. This is a rocky eminence with more form than its slightly higher neighbour, Kaweka J. Ambitious parties may scramble down the aptly named Pinnacle Spur to intercept the Kaweka Flats Track, but most simply retrace their footsteps back down Makahu Spur.

Kiwi Saddle

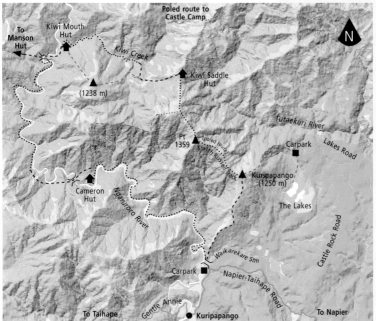

Duration: 2–3 days.

Grade: Medium–Hard.

Times: Kiwi Saddle Hut (8 bunks, wood stove, Category 3): 3.5–4 hours. Kiwi Saddle to Kiwi Mouth Hut (4 bunks, open fire, Category 3) via Kiwi Creek: 2.5–3 hours; via track: 3 hours. Kiwi Mouth Hut to Cameron Hut (6 bunks, open fire, Category 3): 3–4 hours. Cameron Hut to road: 3– 4 hours.

Maps: U20 Kaweka, Kaweka Forest Park Map.

Access: From Napier or Taihape, drive to Kuripapango on the Napier–Taihape Road. About 3 km east of Kuripapango is the Cameron carpark and picnic areas and the start of the track to Kiwi Saddle Hut.

Alternative: It's possible to shorten the trip by dropping down to Cameron Hut along a track that branches off near Kiwi Saddle Hut.

Information: DoC Napier, Ph 06 834 3111.

This interesting weekend tramp in the southern part of the Kaweka Forest Park offers a variety of terrain, with some ridge travel, good views and a day in the mighty Ngaruroro River. Those with angling inclinations may like to carry a portable rod as the Ngaruroro River is one of the best fly-fishing rivers in the North Island, renowned for its large rainbow trout. However, beware of tramping the turbulent Ngaruroro when in flood; it is not a river to be taken lightly. The route described here links three huts, completing a tidy circuit that begins and ends near Kuripapango on the Napier–Taihape Road.

Kuripapango, like other inland Hawkes Bay settlements, is now a mere shadow of its former self. In the late 19th and early 20th centuries it was an important staging point on the road connecting Hawkes Bay with Taihape. For a brief period, it was also a fashionable recreation retreat for Hawkes Bay folk, when it had two sizeable hotels. Completion of the main trunk line in 1905 dramatically reduced traffic through the area, and the road to Kuripapango remains winding and metalled even today.

From the Cameron carpark, a rough 4WD track leads down to the Ngaruroro River, where you cross the Waikarekare Stream on a footbridge. From here, a track begins a steep 750-metre climb through manuka and koromiko forest and beyond to

Mt Kuripapango.

The forests here are largely regenerating after a long history of fires and grazing, which for a while left the area largely bereft of any vegetation. In 1848, missionary-explorer William Colenso commented that the country was of the 'utmost desolate description'. These days, once you emerge above the bushline, views of the landscape still reveal significant scars, but it's not without beauty. The regeneration of native forest is encouraging, even if parts of this are threatened by the spread of wilding pine. Bluebells, foxgloves, eyebrights and *Dracophyllum recurvum* prove attractive here when in flower, and can be enjoyed as the track takes on a slightly easier gradient.

The track sidles just below Mt Kuripapango (1250 metres) and onto the ridge to the northwest. Good views unfold of the eroded Kaweka Range to the north, the tip of the Ruahine Range to the south and the more distant peaks of the volcanic interior. Far below, the Ngaruroro snakes in graceful curves, sometimes almost doubling back on itself.

A gradual climb to Pt 1359 ensues, from where the undulating track leads past a turn-off to Cameron Hut and finally onto a scree descent to Kiwi Saddle. Sitting in a patch of mountain beech on the bush edge is the tidy eight-bunk Kiwi Saddle Hut. The original hut was constructed here in 1947 by the Hastings-based Heretaunga Tramping

Misty dawn over Ngaruroro River, near Kiwi Mouth

Club, which also built and maintains the current one. Beyond the hut, marked tracks lead across a mixture of beech and manuka to a junction where there's a choice of two routes to Kiwi Mouth Hut: the wet-weather track over Pt 1238 or the route down Kiwi Creek. Unless the weather dictates otherwise, the latter is by far the best option as it's both quicker and easier.

A short track drops sharply to Kiwi Creek, which winds between steep banks covered in mountain beech. Although numerous crossings are required, travel down to the confluence with the Ngaruroro River is straightforward, and you may see New Zealand falcon en route. At the confluence lies the four-bunk Kiwi Mouth Hut, used by a mixture of anglers, hunters, trampers and the occasional rafting party. It's a good place to spend the night.

From the hut, a track leads downstream on the true left of the Ngaruroro River, past a swingbridge that crosses to the Manson Hut track, and beyond for about a kilometre until it ends, depositing you in the river bed. The Ngaruroro River is of a considerable size here, having drained most of the western catchments of Kaweka Forest Park and some of the southeastern Kaimanawa Range too. It has numerous rapids, some large, deep pools and a few sections of sizeable boulders. Travel downriver is only possible in good weather, and even then you will need to be familiar with river-crossing techniques. Tramping the Ngaruroro involves making numerous crossings, hopping over shingle beds beside the river and elbowing through forested shortcuts between river bends.

Tramper admires beech forest near Mt Kuripapanga, Kaweka Forest Park

About halfway down, it's possible to use a track that sidles along the true right bank to avoid a section of large rapids, then crosses a swingbridge to the true left. At times of normal river flow, however, this section is negotiable without using the track. A short distance downstream lies Cameron Hut, which makes a convenient lunch stop. Still remaining are a few hours of river travel, but on a sunny summer's day this presents no chore – there are plenty of places for swimming and on occasions you may see blue duck. The first sign that you're near the end is a particularly sharp U-bend in the river. A short distance downstream is a cableway and water gauge, from where it's just a 15-minute walk back to the carpark.

Cape Kidnappers Gannet Reserve

HAWKES BAY

Duration: 1 day.

Grade: Easy-Medium.

Time: 5–7 hours return.

Map: W21 Kidnappers.

Access: From the town of Clive on SH 2, follow signs leading for 9 km to Clifton, where there is a carpark and information panel. The nearby campground has a shop and toilets.

Season: Plateau Colony is closed from 30 June until the Wednesday prior to Labour weekend in October. The best time to visit is from early November to late February, when chicks are present.

Alternative: For those who want less walking, commercial operators run trips out to Cape Kidnappers both along the coast and overland through Summerlee Station.

Information: DoC Napier, Ph 06 834 3111.

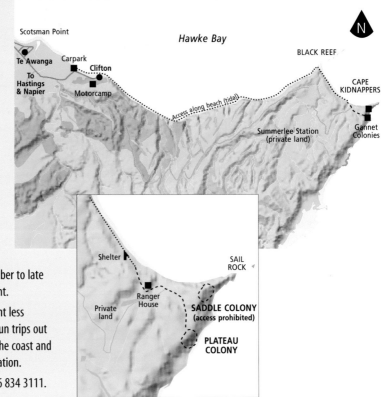

While this trip out to Cape Kidnappers is arguably not a tramp, it does cover some 10 kilometres of dramatic coastal scenery and is of major interest if you like geology and wildlife. It is, of course, most famous for its Australasian gannets (*Morus serrator*), as some 7000 pairs breed here in the largest accessible mainland colony in the world.

Be warned, this is a very popular walk, particularly in December and January – you'll often have to share the beach section with tractors, buses and motorbikes. However, some peace on your walk is possible if you time your trip carefully. You'll need to plan around the low tide as a few sections (notably the cliffs just east of Clifton and at the Black Reef) can't be negotiated at high tide. However, as long as you head out to the cape on an outgoing tide, you can leave only a couple of hours after high tide and beat the masses, especially when this coincides with dawn. Travel is mainly on the gravelly beach, although at mid-tide you'll be forced to boulder-hop closer to the cliffs in places. It's generally fast travel, especially on the sections of hard-packed sand.

Undoubtedly, the cape's layered bluffs form one of the North Island's more impressive coastlines, telling a geological story laid down in clearly visible strata. As well as sandstone, there's a sort of conglomerate and a type of mudstone known as papa. The oldest papa rocks of Cape Kidnappers are some 4–5 million years old, while the sandstones of Black Reef are younger at 2.5 million years old; other deposits closer to Clifton are younger still at less than 1 million years old. The layers represent different deposits laid down as the sea level fluctuated during past ages.

Australasian gannet Morus serrator *and chick, Cape Kidnappers*

After about two hours' walk, the first sign of gannets comes at Black Reef, a series of small islets lying just offshore. In the wrong sort of wind you'll smell the colony here almost before you see it. Black Reef forms a convenient spot from which to observe chicks on the nest, as some are literally at eye-level (you'll have to watch the birds' rather rapid guano expulsion carefully if you don't want to get an eyeful). In contrast to the strikingly handsome adults, with their golden heads and sleek plumage, the chicks are rather ugly, sporting gawky black beaks and white down that looks like a badly stuffed pillow.

Beyond Black Reef there's a view of the sweep of coastline leading to Cape Kidnappers itself and the large sail-shaped island at its easternmost extent. Mud-stone reefs running perpendicular to the shore probe out into the sea between sandy beaches, beyond which a signposted track heads off into some coastal shrubland. The plantings here have been established in recent years by volunteers and DoC in an effort to revegetate part of the cape.

The track leads to a shelter, where there are toilets, a picnic area and some information on the reserve. It's a very pleasant place for lunch, and there's a tank for water too. Beyond the shelter, a well-formed track climbs stiffly to a flat, grassy plateau where the ranger house is situated. Another short climb leads to the Plateau Colony. Here, gannets nest in close proximity to each other, almost in neat, symmetrical lines. You could spend hours here, watching the birds take off to sea, feeding their chicks or clumsily coming in to land. Sharp pecks from their neighbours soon harass those birds that land in the wrong spot until they can scurry back to the correct nest.

Gannets were probably not present at the Cape when Captain Cook named it after an incident on his 1769 voyage, when local Maori attempted to kidnap a Tahitian boy from the *Endeavour*. Naturalist Henry Hill made the first observations of gannets at the cape in the mid-1800s, when there were probably fewer than 50 birds. Hill saw the birds at what is known as the Saddle Colony, situated on a flat section of the narrow ridge that stretches out to the Cape (this colony is closed to the public). The Black Reef and Plateau colonies probably became established in the 1930s.

The gannets return to the colony in August, when they begin nesting and breeding. The first eggs usually hatch in early November. Both parents take turns feeding the ravenous chicks. Small fish – including anchovy, pilchard and yellow-eyed garfish – are the main prey, which the gannets catch from dives that reach speeds of up to 145 kilometres per hour. When they are about four months old, the young birds set off on a remarkable 2800-kilometre flight to Australia. The purpose of the flight is not certain, and some 70–75 per cent of the birds don't survive the arduous crossing. Those that return come back to breed when they are 2–3 years old.

In addition to the gannets, the Plateau Colony offers fine views north across Hawke Bay to Napier, and on a clear day even as far as Mahia Peninsula. Closer is the spectacular Sail Rock, a shark-tooth-shaped island of papa that protrudes out of the Pacific Ocean. Photographs taken in the early 20th century show it used to have a smaller neighbour, which has since been dissolved by the sea.

If you've been lucky enough to arrive at the Cape before the hordes, the return walk is certain to be busier as a multitude of wheeled vehicles arrives to disgorge passengers. But there's a slightly different perspective of the coastline on the way back, and you'll probably have more time to admire places where streams have cut deep canyons in the cliffs or the occasional lonely cabbage trees that stand as sentinels on the tops above.

Gannet colony, Cape Kidnappers

Rangiwahia • Triangle

Duration: 2–3 days.

Grade: Medium.

Times: Table Flat Road to Heritage Lodge (18 bunks, open fire, Category 3): 30 minutes. Heritage Lodge to Iron Gates Hut (8 bunks, wood stove, Category 3): 3–4 hours. Iron Gates to Triangle Hut (6 bunks, wood stove, Category 3): 2.5–3 hours. Triangle Hut to Rangiwahia Hut (12 bunks, gas heater, Category 3): 4–5 hours. Rangiwahia Hut to Renfrew Road: 1.5 hours.

Maps: T22 Mangaweka, U22 Ongaonga, Ruahine Forest Park Map.

Access: From the Manawatu town of Feilding, drive 28 km to Kimbolton on SH 54. Just north of here, turn onto Apiti Road, which soon becomes Oroua Valley Road. After about 12 km Table Flat Road branches off on the right.

Alternative Routes: Both Rangiwahia and Iron Gates Huts make good weekend destinations for those wanting a shorter trip without the need for juggling transport.

Information: DoC Palmerston North, Ph 06 350 9700.

This is a classic Ruahine weekend trip with a mixture of tramping terrain, attractive rivers that offer good swimming, four huts, tussock tops, interesting forests and fine views of the volcanic plateau. Completing the round trip will require a bit of car juggling; alternatively, you could just walk one way to Triangle Hut from either end.

The track starts from Table Flat Road, where there's a carpark with views of Ruapehu and Ngauruhoe, and – on a clear day – even Mt Taranaki. A well-benched track sidles across farmland, down to Umutoi Creek, where an attractive arched bridge leads into Ruahine Forest Park. From here, a gradual climb ensues on what was once an old logging road to a track junction. The left fork leads down to the Oroua River flats and the route upstream, while the right-hand branch heads towards Heritage Lodge and the wet-weather track.

The Oroua River flats provide good camping spots, and travel up-valley from here follows the Oroua River itself. This is not a route for those who aren't confident about river travel and should only be tackled when the water level is low. On a hot summer's day, however, this is great tramping, punctuated by an occasional dip in one of the many pools upstream.

The alternative wet-weather track takes about the same time and follows a well-benched track up-valley, often sidling quite high above the river. A few minutes past the track junction on the wet-weather track lies Heritage Lodge, a large structure with 18 bunks that was built and is maintained by the Manawatu branch of the New Zealand Deerstalkers Association. The lodge makes a good destination in itself for anyone wanting a very short trip, or as an introduction to tramping for young children.

The western side of the Ruahine Range is botanically more diverse than the east, where fairly uniform beech forests dominate. In the west, higher rainfall supports varied podocarp/hardwood forests, including some attractive groves of kaikawaka. Rimu, miro, kamahi and mahoe are

Trampers on Whanahuia Range

just some of the trees encountered along the wet-weather track – luckily, the loggers stopped at about Heritage Lodge.

The track dips to cross a few substantial tributaries of the Oroua, of which Tunupo Creek is the most boisterous (as there's no bridge here, it could present a problem when in flood). Iron Gates Hut lies on a grassy terrace above the Oroua River, reached around three or four hours from Heritage Lodge.

Upstream of Iron Gates Hut, the tramping becomes more difficult. Triangle Hut lies past a formidable gorge in the Oroua River and can only be reached in reasonable weather and with low water levels. The reward for travel here is the chance to encounter blue ducks, and a growing sense that you are deep in the heart of the Ruahine mountains. At first there's a few boulder-strewn river crossings, past an island in the river, then a short, sharp climb over a prominent spur to avoid the most tortuous section of the gorge. The start of this track is marked by a large orange triangle on the true right of a tributary (not the true left, as marked on the topographical map).

Upstream, the route meanders back and forth across the river, requiring numerous crossings. In places, the forest overhangs, lending the stream an almost sylvan feel. Higher up, near Triangle Hut, large floods have swept the banks clear of live vegetation and strewn logs about, testimony to both the power of rivers in high flow and the large catchment of the Oroua.

Triangle Hut sits back from the river, also on a grassy terrace and near a prominent river fork. If this is your first day, you'll probably want to stop here for the night, but those taking a more leisurely three days may want to contemplate camping on the tops of the Whanahuia Range. Opposite Triangle Hut, a track ascends steeply through beech forest, which merges into kaikawaka and leatherwood near the bush-line. Once through the subalpine scrub, you finally emerge onto tussock.

Poles lead towards Pt 1635 but then sidle off to a broad, flat saddle where there are reasonable campsites and some nearby tarns for water. On a calm, fine evening this is a great spot to contemplate very little other than the changes in the colour of the sky over the nearby ranges.

From the tarns, the track climbs steadily up a well-defined path onto a knob just before Mangahuia (1583 metres). From here, there are broad views of the Ruahine Range, stretching from Te Hekenga down to Tunupo, as well as the more distant peaks of the volcanic plateau.

Past a signpost, a gentle three-kilometre stroll leads down the well-poled tussock ridge towards the bushline, and Rangiwahia Hut. The original hut – an old shepherd's shelter constructed in 1930 – was expanded by the newly formed Rangiwahia Ski Club in 1938. The club winched a bulldozer up a spur to level some slopes, and installed a rope tow that was powered by an Indian motorbike! Skiing was popular here for a brief period, and the club peaked at 80 members. It disbanded after World War II. The New Zealand Forest Service built the second hut in 1967 and also construct-ed the current one in 1982. Despite suitable topography, in these days of warmer winters and poorer snowfall the area has limited ski potential, but a really good dump does entice the occasional ski tourer.

From Rangiwahia Hut you are once again on a well-graded track, which soon descends through subalpine scrub and kaikawaka forest to another attractive arched bridge, this one spanning an impressively narrow chasm some 70 metres deep. Beyond, the track sidles out to Renfrew Road and is easy going apart from a detour where the original track has dangerously slipped away. This slip is still active, and sometimes it's necessary to use the alternative Deadmans Track (the first ridge to the south).

Whanahuia Range at dawn

Sawtooth Ridge

Duration: 2–3 days.

Grade: Hard.

Times: Mill Road to Daphne Hut (12 bunks, wood stove, Category 3) via Tukituki River: 2.5–3 hours. Daphne Hut to Howletts Hut (8 bunks, wood stove, Category 3): 2 hours. Howletts Hut to Tarn Biv (2 bunks, Category 4) via Sawtooth Ridge: 5–6 hours. Tarn Biv to Tukituki River and roadend via Rosvalls Track: 3–4 hours.

Map: U22 Ongaonga.

Access: From SH50, some 10 km south of Ongaonga, turn onto Makaretu Road. After 4 km turn left onto Mill Road and follow this until you halt at a locked gate on a farm, near a woolshed. The legal access to the Tukituki River begins about 200 m further along this road, where a DoC and Fish & Game sign indicates the start of the track.

Alternative Routes: It's also possible to reach Daphne Hut from a track that starts from Kashmir Road.

Information: DoC Ongaonga, Ph 06 856 6808; DoC Napier, Ph 06 834 3111.

From some profiles the Sawtooth Ridge looks as formidable a prospect as its name suggests, but in reality this section of the Ruahine Range is not that steep, and in everything but windy or winter conditions it is well within the abilities of most experienced trampers. The tramp begins from the Tukituki River, climbs to Howletts Hut and then traverses the Sawtooth to Tarn Biv, from where it descends back to the river. For those not wishing to tackle the ridge itself, all three huts on this round trip make worthwhile destinations in their own right.

From the DoC sign at the end of Mill Road, follow a poled route down an old road to the Tukituki River, which ends about ten minutes downstream of the confluence with Moorcock Stream. To start with, the gravelly river is not particularly attractive, but it does provide fast travel upstream. After about 30 minutes, you reach a sign-posted junction marking the end of Rosvalls Track.

Upstream, the Tukituki becomes more boulder-strewn, and beech forest begins to crowd in over the banks. After a further two hours, past an attractive stand of rimu trees, you reach another signposted junction where a track leads off to Kashmir Road (the alternative entry point). Just upriver, the Tukituki enters a small gorge that can be difficult to pass in times of flood. Once through the gorge, the river opens to a stream junction where three prominent spurs meet. You'll climb one of these to reach Howletts Hut, but first it's worth taking a break at nearby Daphne Hut. The hut lies on a small flat about 100 metres upstream on the Tukituki's true left. It has an unusual A-frame design and was built in 1986 by the Takapau Lions Club.

Sawtooth Ridge

The track up Daphne Spur starts steeply, like most of those in the V-shaped river valleys of the North Island mountain axis. After climbing for 200 metres, it eases off a little and the spur begins to narrow as you tramp steadily upwards. In places, the track is quite eroded, and there are some big steps for those with short legs! After a brief section through subalpine scrub, the track gains Daphne Ridge, where Howletts Hut lies in a sheltered hollow overlooking the north branch of the Tukituki.

This is a grand spot with commanding views, and it comes as no surprise to learn that a number of different huts have occupied the site. A Hawkes Bay schoolteacher and botanist, William Howlett, built the original hut in 1893 out of split mountain cedar. It lasted until about 1930, then in 1938 construction of a replacement hut was begun by the then Ruahine Tramping Club (Palmerston North) and the Heretaunga Tramping Club (Hawkes Bay). This hut was opened in 1940. The current hut was built by the latter club in 1978/79, with minor improvements since. Like Daphne, Howletts has an unusual design, but it is very comfortable – especially on a winter's night with the potbelly stove glowing.

The Sawtooth Ridge can't be seen clearly from Howletts Hut – it first comes into view about an hour along Daphne Ridge. After leaving the hut, a rough track passes through a brief section of stunted forest then sidles around scree and tussock slopes (there's a tarn for water near here). A steady climb up tussock slopes ensues, leading onto a knoll beneath Tiraha. From here, the Sawtooth does indeed look impressive, its broken spine dropping sharply into very steep, eroded gullies. During winters past, when cold weather was more reliable, climbers used to practise their ice-climbing skills in these gullies.

As the direct approach to Tiraha is very steep, most trampers opt to reach it by first sidling onto a small tussock spur that branches off to the southeast. From Tiraha (1668 metres and marked by a large cairn), the Sawtooth Ridge lies spread out before you, no longer looking much like a saw, or at most a very blunt one. Although steep-sided, the actual ridge crest is quite rounded, and any narrow sections are easily negotiated by well-defined sidles. Still, in windy conditions it can prove nerve-racking, and a traverse in winter requires sound mountaineering skills.

The steepest sections all come in the first one-and-a-half kilometres, and most can be passed by sidling to the east. Where the ridge is narrower, the track is quite well defined and intermittent cairns mark the way. On the flatter sections beyond, you begin a climb up to Ohuinga (1686 metres). Note that first you reach a bump that might be mistaken for Ohuinga – the real one is further north. From Ohuinga, three ridges branch off, and in misty conditions getting the right one onto Black Ridge (which heads southeast) may require taking a compass bearing. A steep drop leads to a saddle, followed by a climb around a couple of knolls that finally leads onto undulating, tarn-studded slopes. These make the ideal spot for an extended lunch break. Black Ridge provides views of perhaps the most impressive profile of the Sawtooth, and now you can relax in the knowledge that the hard part is over.

Sunrise at Howlett's Hut

At the end of Black Ridge is the recently renovated Tarn Biv, a tidy two-bunk dog-box with an open-air longdrop. From here, a well-marked track leads through gnarled mountain beech forest to a rocky knoll (1285 metres) where there is a signposted track junction. One track leads straight down to Daphne Hut, while the other, Rosvalls Track, drops directly to the Tukituki River further east. Rosvalls provides the quickest route back to your car. While the top section of the track has recently been cleared, the lower section is rather overgrown, but it is still easy enough to follow providing you look out for the markers. Once back in the Tukituki Valley, simply retrace your previous day's route back to the farm and your vehicle.

Sunrise Hut • Waipawa Saddle

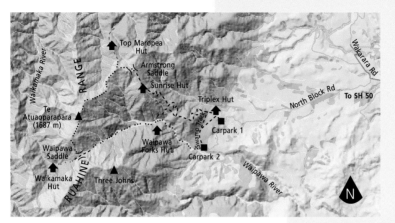

Duration: 2 days.

Grade: Medium.

Times: North Block Road to Waipawa Forks Hut (12 bunks, wood stove, Category 3): 1 hour. Waipawa Forks Hut to Waipawa Saddle: 2 hours. Waipawa Saddle to Sunrise Hut (10 bunks, gas heater, cooking rings, Category 2): 3–4 hours. Sunrise Hut to Triplex Hut (12 bunks, wood stove, Category 3): 2–2.5 hours. Triplex Hut to roadend via Swamp Track: 30 minutes.

Map: U22 Ongaonga.

Access: From SH50 just north of Ongaonga, turn left onto Wakarara Road. Follow this to Wakarara, where you turn left onto North Block Road. There are two carparks on North Block Road; the first is signposted for access to Triplex Hut. Drive past this one, and continue through some farm gates to the second carpark, just above the Waipawa River.

Information: DoC Ongaonga, Ph 06 856 6808; DoC Napier, Ph 06 834 3111.

Sunrise Hut occupies one of the best tops locations in the Ruahine Range, and as it is serviced by a high-quality track, it remains one of the most popular destinations in the park. While the hut is a fine destination in its own right, those wanting a slightly more challenging round trip can reach it via the Waipawa River and Te Atuaoparapara.

From the second carpark on North Block Road, follow an old vehicle track down to the Waipawa River. Between floods, the lower Waipawa River is regularly choked with introduced lupin, which, while attractive in flower, can otherwise detract from the start of the tramp. However, travel proves easy on the shingly riverbed, and progress is swift up into more wild reaches of the valley.

There's one small, narrow section of the river, too feeble to call a gorge, but a possible obstacle if the river is in flood. Waipawa Forks Hut is a 12-bunk hut, situated on a high ledge five minutes above the true left of the river. Watch out for the short track leading up to it as the hut is not visible from the riverbed.

Shortly upstream from the hut, on the opposite side of the valley, is a track leading to Sunrise Hut. If the weather proves unsuitable for tops travel, this would make a good alternative route to the one described here. Otherwise, carry on climbing gradually up the Waipawa River, with the distinctive scoop of the Waipawa Saddle visible on the skyline ahead. Further up, the river becomes boulder-strewn, and subalpine scrub begins to close in on the banks. The final push to the saddle follows a

Sunrise Hut, Ruahine Forest Park

well-worn track, which climbs a spur through a fairly dense band of leatherwood.

A cairn and two waratahs mark the saddle, and there are views westwards over to the Hikurangi Range and the Ruahine interior. A short side-trip, worth doing in summer, is an amble down to the headwaters of the Waikamaka River, perhaps as far as Waikamaka Hut. Initially steep and poled, the route soon drops into the riverbed. This proves to be a delightful valley, where *Ranunculus insignis* buttercups grow in profusion, often right by the stream edge.

Back at Waipawa Saddle, a sharp climb ensues up scree and alpine tussock slopes, without anything much in the way of cairns. Higher up, views unfold east over Hawkes Bay and north to the mountains of Tongariro National Park. There's a flat shelf here, with ample tarns for drinking water and a few places for camping. The diversity of alpine plants warrants a closer look – there's North Island edelweiss, eyebrights, at least two sorts of *Celmisia* daisies and the attractive rust-coloured *Ranunculus recurvum*.

Te Atuaoparapara has by now come into sharp profile, looking rather more precipitous than it actually is. To reach it, you initially drop down past some tarns to a small dip in the range, then begin a short but steep slog up scree slopes, keeping well to the west of the ridge crest. A small trig station marks the top.

From here, your route to Sunrise Hut is clear: a big drop down to a scrubby saddle, then an undulating climb over a knob to Armstrong Saddle and the final stretch to Buttercup Hollow. The first part of the descent from Te Atuaoparapara is quite well defined, but once you are in the scrub it becomes less so, and travel is mostly a matter of finding tussock leads through the patches of leatherwood. On the far side, where the ridge becomes defined again, a quite pronounced route leads up to a sign-posted knoll. Here, a side-route branches off to Top Maropea Hut. Continue past the junction down to Armstrong Saddle.

On the saddle, an interpretation panel describes the area's history. Back in July 1935, pioneer aviator Hamish Armstrong disappeared while on a flight from Dannevirke to Hastings. Some two weeks into an intensive search his wrecked Gypsy Moth was found crashed on the saddle. However, no trace of Armstrong was found, excepting a shirt bearing the brand name Triplex. Presumably, he survived the crash sufficiently uninjured to try to walk out but never made it.

A short stroll along a track that skirts some of the most impressive erosion scars in the country leads to the Lockwood-style Sunrise Hut. It's perched in the sheltered Buttercup Hollow with commanding views eastwards, and there are a couple of campsites nearby. From the hut, a well-benched track leads down a prominent spur to the lowland forest below, and eventually to Triplex Hut. There are tree ferns aplenty, attractive red beech forest, some mountain cabbage trees and the occasional mistletoe protected by possum barriers. In recent years the track has been upgraded to make it ideal for family groups and less experienced trampers. About halfway down you reach a track that branches off south to Waipawa Forks Hut, which provides an alternative route back to your vehicle.

Most walkers, however, will want to continue to Triplex Hut (where there is ample room for camping)

Tarn below Te Atuaoparapara, Ruahine Forest Park

and return along the pleasant Swamp Track. Here, podocarp trees – including miro, kahikatea and rimu – intersperse with beech forest to give some sense of the lowland forests that once dominated much of Hawkes Bay. Listen out for kakariki and New Zealand falcon.

Mid Pohangina Hut

Duration: 2 days.

Grade: Medium.

Times: Tamaki West Road to Stanfield Hut (8 bunks, wood stove, Category 3) via river: 1.5 hours; via Holmes Ridge: 2 hours. Stanfield to Cattle Creek Hut (8 bunks, wood stove, Category 3): 2 hours. Cattle Creek to Mid Pohangina Hut (4 bunks, open fire, Category 3): 2–3 hours. Mid Pohangina to Pohangina Valley East Road: 4–6 hours.

Maps: T23 Kimbolton, U23 Dannevirke, Ruahine Forest Park Map.

Access: From SH2 just south of Dannevirke, take Law Road to Ruaroa and then turn right onto Top Grass Road. Branch left onto Tamaki West Road after about 3 km; there's a carpark, toilet, camping and picnic area at the roadend. The other end of the route is accessed on Pohangina Valley East Road, north of Ashhurst.

Alternative routes: During periods of low flow it's possible to splash down the Pohangina River from Mid Pohangina Hut all the way out to farmland. This makes a great summer alternative, but it does take longer and requires negotiating some deep holes in gorged sections of the river.

Information: DoC Palmerston North, Ph 06 350 9700.

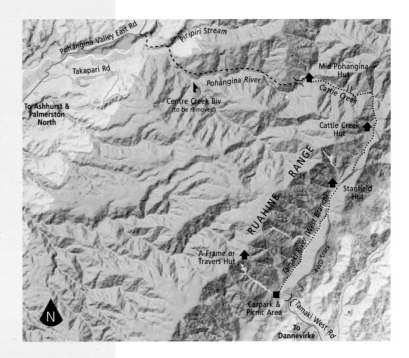

This tramp crosses the Ruahines at the lowest pass on the entire range, linking the Tamaki River on the east with Cattle Creek and the Pohangina River in the west. There are three huts, plenty of places for swimming, and it's probably the most painless way of completing a Ruahine crossing. It's also one of the few traverses possible in a weekend where the transport is not too difficult to organise.

From the end of Tamaki West Road, you can either tramp up the riverbed of the Tamaki River west branch or take the Holmes Ridge Track. If water levels are low, the river is the best option, as it's an easy amble up-valley on the gravelly riverbed, crossing where necessary. In places, introduced lupin and *Buddleia* infest the banks, but floods regularly gouge them out. Beyond the junction with the end of the Holmes Ridge Track, reached after about an hour, a formed track leads for 30 minutes to Stanfield Hut. Unfortunately, the hut suffers from occasional vandalism, being so close to the roadend, but you'll probably want to push on to Cattle Creek Hut anyway. A short distance upstream, a track begins a solid climb to a low, forested saddle on the Ruahine Range.

From the saddle, there are two possible routes to Cattle Creek Hut: via a track along a low section of the Ruahine Range, or down into the headwaters of Cattle Creek. While the latter is open and gravelly, the ridge route is probably more pleasant. It follows a track that leads through kamahi, totara and rata forest – along with some patches of leatherwood – for about two kilometres before reaching a junction where it leaves the main range and drops sharply down to Cattle Creek and the hut. This tidy hut lies on a terrace on the true left bank, just downstream of the point where the track emerges onto the river. Sadly, the devastation brought by possums to the forest in this part of the Ruahines is all too evident, with many canopy trees dead or dying.

The next day, you follow Cattle Creek to its junction with the Pohangina River; this section is really the highlight of the trip, particularly on a warm summer's day. Initially, the river provides easy travel on gravel and boulders. After about an hour you reach a sizeable pool that you can either scramble around or swim through (which can be quite pleasant when it's hot). Further downstream, the creek enters a small but difficult gorge, where a waterfall halts progress. Getting past this obstacle involves negotiating a steep rocky bank on the true left using a chain rope installed by DoC.

After this rather exhilarating descent, another hour or so of river travel leads to a fairly large slip on the true right. It's possible to take a shortcut to Mid Pohangina Hut, crossing an obvious saddle near this

Tramper crosses swingbridge over Pohangina River

slip. The hut is a very tidy four-bunker, set amongst some tall rimu trees. Alternatively, you can bypass the hut and continue down Cattle Creek to its junction with the Pohangina River.

The Pohangina is a sizeable Ruahine river with a large catchment and is well-known for blue ducks. Several pairs occupy territories for most of the river's length, and recent research suggests that the Ruahines are one of the few places where numbers of this endangered waterfowl are actually increasing.

There's a swingbridge over the river about 300 metres upstream of the Cattle Creek confluence, leading onto the sidle track down-valley. The impressively green pools below the swingbridge are deep and ideal for swimming. It takes a full day to travel down through the gorges of the Pohangina River from Mid Pohangina Hut, with one pool to swim en route and another waterfall to negotiate below Centre Creek, and it's definitely a fine-weather trip only. However, in the right conditions the lower Pohangina provides classic river tramping.

The sidle track is really the only option in wet weather, and despite the ups and downs it provides much faster travel. From the swingbridge, the track climbs for a while before settling into some benched travel through mahoe, horopito and podocarp forest. Watch for ongaonga in the shadier sections. On occasions, there are good viewpoints over the river, revealing some of the valley's impressive slips.

Several small streams are crossed before the track reaches a junction where a side trail leads down to the rather dilapidated Centre Creek Biv (DoC plans to remove this biv, which will be no great loss unless you're really keen on hut bagging). Travel becomes easier as the valley opens out, eventually crossing Piripiri Stream on the edge of the farmland. Poles lead across river terraces, over the Te Ano Whiro Stream, then up a sharp farm track – fairly unwelcome at this end of the day – that climbs to the carpark at the Pakohu Scenic Reserve on Pohangina Valley East Road.

Mid Pohangina Hut, Pohangina valley

Ascent Mangaweka

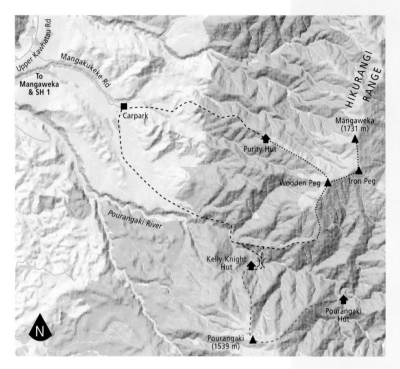

Duration: 2 days.

Grade: Medium.

Times: Mangakukeke Road to Purity Hut (3 bunks, open fire, Category 4): 2–3 hours. Purity to Wooden Peg: 1.5 hours. Wooden Peg to Mangaweka summit: 1 hour return. Wooden Peg to Kelly Knight Hut (8 bunks, wood stove, Category 3): 2–3 hours. Kelly Knight to road 2-3 hours.

Maps: U22 Ongaonga, T22 Mangaweka, Ruahine Forest Park Map.

Access: Turn off SH1 at Mangaweka onto SH54. Past the Rangitikei Bridge, turn left onto the Kawhatau Valley Road. Follow this past Upper Kawhatau, then turn right onto Mangakukeke Road, where there's a carpark, toilet and information panel. The exit from Kelly Knight Hut crosses private farmland; to use this route, you must first gain permission from the nearby farmhouse on the right (Bayfield Farm, Ph 06 382 5577). Note that this access is normally restricted during calving (July – September).

Alternative routes: From Purity Hut it's also possible to traverse the Hikurangi Range past McKinnon Hut to the Kawhatau River, but this is not a round trip and so requires organising appropriate transport.

Information: DoC Palmerston North, Ph 06 350 9700.

Mangaweka (1731 metres) is the highest point on the Ruahine Range, and is accessible from Purity Hut over a weekend trip. As well as two huts, some impressive rolling tussock tops and excellent views, this tramp also passes through some of the best stands of kaikawaka forest in the park. It's a good trip to make in northerly weather, as this inland part of the Ruahines often stays cloudy but dry when areas further north or west are wet. All in all, it is a satisfying round trip, especially for those who like peak-bagging.

From the carpark at Mangakukeke Road, a series of marker poles leads over muddy farmland, crossing one stream and then rising sharply beside a fence-line onto a spur. Once you are on the spur proper, you've reached the Ruahine Forest Park boundary and the gradient eases off somewhat for the rest of the climb up to Purity Hut. Red and silver beech dominate at first, with prickly shield fern on the forest floor. Higher up, the first of the kaikawaka trees makes an appearance, and twenty minutes later you're surrounded by a magnificent grove of them at Purity Hut. The three-bunk hut is small and rustic, and while providing adequate shelter, it does get very cold on winter nights.

Kaikawaka forest, Pourangaki valley

Shortly above Purity Hut you reach the bushline, where a route pushes upwards through fairly lush tussock on a well-defined spur leading to the Hikurangi Range. By the time you reach Wooden Peg, most of the climbing is done, and it's only a gentle stroll to the rounded summit of Mangaweka. Here, the views are panoramic, encapsulating the entire northern extent of the Ruahine Range as well as glimpses of distant Taranaki and Ruapehu.

The route towards the Pourangaki River from Wooden Peg is partially poled, and as the spur is not well-defined these markers prove very welcome in misty conditions. During the descent to the bushline, tussock hides occasional speargrass that seemingly lies in wait to stab you. The number of poles increases near the bushline, where there are some patches of leatherwood to push through and one steep scree slope to negotiate. In summer, tarns here provide water.

Once it enters the subalpine scrub, the track becomes well-marked, leading down into another stand of kaikawaka forest. The flaking, rust-coloured bark of these trees contrasts strongly with the mossy green undergrowth, providing an enchanting place for a rest. Further down the spur, mountain beech and the occasional totara eventually replace the kaikawaka. The track descends at a fairly gentle gradient, before reaching a track junction marked by a cairn. Continue straight ahead down the spur if you don't want to visit Kelly Knight Hut, or turn sharp left if you do.

This latter section of track drops steeply down a bush face for 150 metres before intersecting the main Pourangaki Valley Track. Follow this up-valley a short distance, then cross a swingbridge over the Pourangaki River and walk a couple of hundred metres down the other side to a grassy flat where Kelly Knight Hut is situated. The tidy eight-bunk hut was built in 1975, upgraded in 1992, and is named after local hunter Kelly Knight. The lower altitude and wood stove ensure it's a much cosier place than Purity Hut!

The tramp out follows the well-graded and benched Pourangaki Valley Track, on the true right of the river. At one point there are good views of a narrow section of the river, but mostly you stroll through red beech forest that is punctuated by the occasional rimu. One-and-a-half hours from the hut, you emerge on the private land of Bayfield Farm (see Access notes on page 113), where a flat 10-minute stroll over paddocks leads to a vehicle track and the carpark.

OPPOSITE: Hikurangi Range in winter

Matemateaonga Walkway

Duration: 3–4 days.

Grade: Easy–Medium.

Times: Kohi Saddle to Omaru Hut (12 bunks, wood stove, Category 2): 1.5–2 hours. Omaru to Mt Humphries turn-off: 3 hours. Ascent Mt Humphries: 1.5 hours return. Turn-off to Pouri Hut (18 bunks, wood stove, Category 2): 2 hours. Pouri to Ngapurua Shelter: 4–4.5 hours. Ngapurua to Puketotara Hut (12 bunks, wood stove, Category 2): 3.5 hours. Puketotara to Whanganui River: 1 hour.

Map: R20 Matemateaonga.

Access: Turn off SH3 at Stratford onto SH43. Follow this for 30 km until you reach Strathmore. Turn right and follow the road for 8 km to the junction of Upper and Lower Mangaehu roads. Turn left here (towards Aotuhia), from where it's 16 km to Kohi Saddle and the start of the track. Prior to departure, you'll need to arrange a jetboat pick-up at the eastern end of the track on the Whanganui River. Some companies can arrange your transport for both ends.

Information: DoC Wanganui, Ph 06 345 2402.

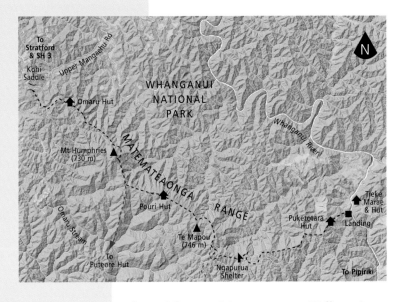

The 42-kilometre Matemateaonga Walkway is an old Maori route that traverses the heart of the North Island's second-largest expanse of native forest, that of Whanganui National Park and the neighbouring Waitotara Conservation Area. The track begins a considerable distance inland from the Taranaki town of Stratford and ends somewhere even more remote, right on the banks of the Whanganui River. Although the walk can be accomplished in as little as two days, most parties require at least another day or two, given the difficult and time-consuming transport arrangements.

From Kohi Saddle, a large sign and stile indicate the start of the walkway, which is often very muddy until a second stile is crossed onto the track proper. It's a pleasure to walk on this well-benched track which follows a remarkably even gradient along the Matemateaonga Range. Nowhere (excepting the short side-trip to Mt Humphries) does the track climb more than about 20 metres, a fact made less surprising once you realise it follows the original route of a never-completed road. The walkway now runs along what was intended to be the Whakaihuwhaka Road, linking Stratford with the main trunk line at Raetihi. Although a pilot track was cut in 1911, the outbreak of World War I ensured it was never widened, and the road suffered the same fate of many later

116

settlement ventures in the Whanganui area – abandonment.

Aside from the easy gradient, another feature of the Matemateaonga that differentiates it from most other tramps is the presence of small marker posts every kilometre, each indicating the distance to Puketotara Hut. These serve a more useful gauge of your progress than you might imagine, because the flatness of the track means distances translate very well into time.

Omaru Hut lies well-situated only a couple of hours from the roadend and is as far as most parties want to go after the long drive in. Like the rest of those along the walkway, the hut was built in the early 1980s during a rash of enthusiasm that saw several tracks – including the Matemateaonga – upgraded into walkways.

Northern rata tree, Matemateaonga Walkway

If you don't like bush, then the Matemateaonga probably isn't ideal, but for those who appreciate the dense, dark and almost claustrophobic nature of huge forest expanses it's a wonderful walk. Not that the forest is by any means uniform; in fact it's the subtle variations that create interest as you travel. Patches of wheki interrupt the canopy, which is dominated by northern rata and kamahi, with rewarewa, rimu, mahoe and hinau common in places. There are also some attractive stands of tawa, whose leaves form deep litter on the track. On some parts of the forest floor are impressive patches of *Dawsonia superba*, the world's tallest moss.

Roughly halfway between Omaru and Pouri Huts lies the side track to Mt Humphries, at 730 metres the second-highest point in Whanganui National Park. The one-and-a-half hour return trip to the summit is worthwhile for the extensive vista: on a clear day Mt Taranaki and the peaks of Tongariro National Park are all plainly visible, as is the Whanganui River – a topographical tribute to the Maori legend celebrating the links between all these features.

The day between Pouri and Puketotara huts is by far the longest on the tramp, but the conveniently positioned Ngapurua Shelter provides a good place for a lunch break, and there is water here, too. By this stage you are right in the heart of the great forest, and it's really only the ease of the track that disguises your remoteness.

The fairly low, uniform height of the Matemateaonga Range and lack of tops disguise how rugged and remote the surrounding bush country really is. It's actually ancient peneplain, some one million years old, subsequently thrust up to its present height and now cut by numerous rivers, including the Whanganui, Omaru and

Waitotara. Off-track travel is extremely arduous, with papa bluffs and deeply incised gorges to negotiate, not to mention the dense bush.

There are glimpses of this ruggedness from clearings along the track, often from the edge of slips or from numerous bridges that span small creeks. Despite the presence of these creeks, in summer you'd be well advised to carry some water as the track's position near the crest of the range can make it scarce.

Puketotara Hut lies only a couple of kilometres from the track end at the Whanganui River. This is the only section of track that descends notably, down a series of steps, through a couple of grassy clearings, then finally down more steps to a point where you first glimpse the river. The Whanganui itself has a character unique among New Zealand rivers, with papa cliffs, numerous waterfalls and a tangible presence of history. During floods, the water is often a chocolate-milkshake colour, swirling with subdued power, and the level can rise or drop very quickly. Locals consider a six-metre rise to be just a 'fresh'; 'floods' are considerably bigger!

The jetboat ride from the landing out to Pipiriki is undoubtedly one of the high-lights of the trip, providing a snapshot experience of New Zealand's longest navigable river. Although the paddle-steamers may have gone, you are likely to pass some canoeists enjoying downstream travel.

Matemateaonga Walkway

Trains Hut

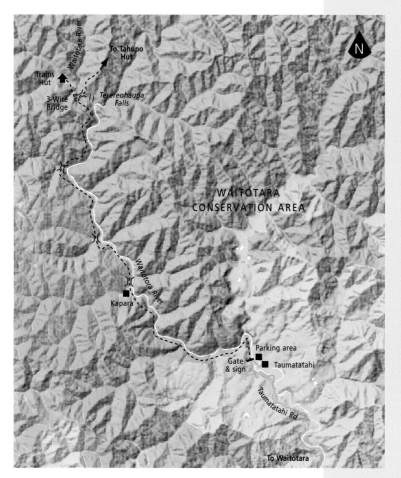

Duration: 2 days.

Grade: Easy.

Times: Taumatatahi to Trains Hut (8 bunks, wood stove, Category 3): 4–6 hours.

Maps: R21 Ngamatapouri, R20 Matemateaonga.

Access: From SH3 at Waitotara, turn onto Waitotara Valley Road. Follow it to Makakaho Junction, then turn left onto Taumatatahi Road. Follow this to the roadend, and park on a grassy area just before a bridge over the Waitotara River. Altogether, it's a long drive of some 57 km, the last 10 km of which is windy and metalled.

Alternative routes: It's also possible to jetboat up the Waitotara River from Taumatatahi, to a point just below the Terereohaupa Falls. The ride can be arranged both ways, or as a 'jetboat in, walk out' trip, through the Taumatatahi-based operator Remote Adventures.

Information: DoC Wanganui, Ph 06 345 2402.

The tramp to Trains Hut in the Waitotara Conservation Area is one of those trips known only to a few Wanganui locals, but it deserves wider attention. From a remote farm in the upper Waitotara Valley, a well-benched track leads beside the Waitotara River to the old homestead at Kapara then on to Trains Hut. The area is interesting for its history, attractive forests and the underlying papa topography. As the hut lies at an altitude of only 100 metres it's never very cold even in winter, and the completely bridged track allows all-weather access. Altogether Trains Hut provides a good all-season destination.

From the grassy flat where you park your car, walk back to the last curve on the road and take the farm road leading through an open gate. Nearby, there's an inconspicuous sign that reads 'Trains Hut 5 hours'. A benched track which used to

Terereohaupa Falls, Waitotara River

exist here was unfortunately bulldozed into a muddy road recently by the South Taranaki District Council, who maintain the route as far as Kapara. At one point you pass an old rail slip – the first sign of past logging activity.

The Waitotara River itself is in some ways a smaller version of its much larger neighbour, the Whanganui, in that it is slow-moving, often brown and rarely without a partially submerged log or two on the bends. Covering the steep banks rising from the river are exceptionally green forests that include a verdant mix of northern rata, rimu, tawa, mahoe and nikau palms. There are North Island robins galore, often calling in their surprisingly loud and seemingly indignant manner.

After an hour or so you come across the dismantled remains of an old woodern bridge. In what I view as an act of vandalism, the South Taranaki District Council destroyed this wonderful old historic bridge, which used to be one of the highlights of the tramp. It was a symbol of past endeavour, which now you can only read about.

Thankfully, due to the efforts of the late Arthur Bates (a Wanganui historian and tramper), the following history has been re-corded. In the early days of the area's farming settlement prior to the 1890s, transport was by horse or canoe. Later, a road was pushed through to its present end. One of the set-tlers, a South African Boer named William Van Asch, had taken up a remote holding at Kapara, and through the force of his personality managed to convince the authorities to extend the road to his homestead which lay a further six kilometres through wilder-ness. It's this old road that the track now follows, and the wooden bridge presumably dated from that era too.

You soon reach Kapara, at the junction of the Waitotara and one of its tributar-ies, where lie the remains of the homestead. Although Van Asch felled a considerable area of bush for his farm and built his own sawmill, he was obviously a man with some conservation ideals. He sold Kapara in 1912 but continued to be active in the region's politics. Thanks to his campaigning, a huge block of bush lying to the north of the Waitotara was designated a 'climatic reserve', reversing an earlier decision to divide it into sections. Thus was formed the basis for what is now the Waitotara Conservation Area.

The Kapara homestead is now largely in ruins, with a sagging and leaky roof, and it retains little of its former grandeur as a large house with an extensive garden and even a tennis court. It now looks forlorn and speaks volumes about hardship, ruin and lost dreams. Although the land is still private property, trampers can legally cross it on the designated track.

From Kapara, the track leads north towards the river and drops to cross a stream via a footbridge. This is the first of a number of gulches incised in the highly erodable papa that underlies the whole area. At this stage the track noticeably improves as you enter the Waitotara Conservation Area, which is under the management of DoC. Travel is pleasant along the well-benched track which passes through regenerating forest dominated by manuka and wheki. Several footbridges cross small streams, while two swingbridges cross larger ones. A reasonable grassy campsite appears about 15 minutes past the second swingbridge. On this section you're likely to encounter several wild goats, the scourge of the area and a major conservation problem.

About 15 minutes before Trains Hut, you pass the Terereohaupa Falls, an attractive cascade falling in a silky veil over an undercut papa bluff. Accessible on this side of the river is a good swimming hole beneath the falls. However those wanting an even better viewpoint to admire the cascade will need to access the opposite bank. This requires crossing a three-wire bridge located five minutes upstream, followed by a scramble downstream on an overgrown track for 15-20 minutes.

Like Kapara, the area around Trains Hut was once farmed, and the hut sits in a grassy clearing dotted with wheki. The hut is named after Fred Train, a Waitotara storekeeper, who was given the surrounding land in payment for a debt owed by the original settler. Train's sons tried to farm the area but left in 1922. According to Arthur

Old bridge, Waitotara Valley. This historic wooden bridge pictured in 2001, about a year before it was dismantled.

Bates, the original Trains Hut even made headlines in the national newspapers once. The news concerned a plane crash, echoing the one that occurred at Armstrong Saddle in the Ruahines (see Sunrise Hut, p. 107), although fortunately this one ended happily.

In December 1949, Oswald and Ian Palmer (a father and son) crashed their Tiger Moth during a flight from Wanganui to New Plymouth. After the subsequent search they were given up for dead, but to the surprise of everyone the pair emerged out of the bush at Kapara 16 days after the accident. They'd survived the first six days' walk on three packets of chewing gum and were relieved to find food left by hunters at Trains Hut. After a rest at the hut, they summoned sufficient energy to continue to Kapara.

The current Trains Hut was built in 1990, and while not a great location, its porch does make a convenient place from which to listen for North Island brown kiwi at night. The following day you can retrace your footsteps, unless you've made arrangements for a jetboat pick-up from below the falls.

Waitotara River, Waitotara Forest

Northern Crossing

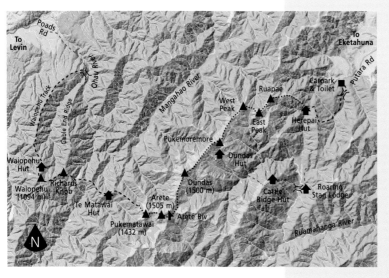

Duration: 2–3 days.

Grade: Hard.

Times: Putara Road to Herepai Hut (10 bunks, wood stove, Category 3): 2 hours. Herepai to Dundas Hut (6 bunks, Category 3): 5–7 hours. Dundas to Arete Biv (2 bunks, Category 4): 3 hours. Arete to Te Matawai Hut (20 bunks, wood stove, Category 3): 2.5 hours. Te Matawai to Waiopehu Hut (18 bunks, wood stove, Category 3): 3 hours. Waiopehu to Poads Road: 3 hours.

Maps: S25 Levin, Tararua Forest Park Map.

Access: Turn off SH2 at Eketahuna, following signs to Putara; these lead you onto Nireaha Road and Priests Road, and finally to Putara Road.

Alternative routes: From Te Matawai Hut it's possible to drop down to the Ohau River via the Yeates Track. This takes less time than the route described, but is a dry-weather route only (see Mangahao Flats, p. 127). Waiopehu Hut makes a much shorter, though superb, destination for a weekend tramp.

Information: DoC Waikanae, Ph 04 296 1112; DoC Masterton, Ph 06 377 0022.

The Tararua Northern Crossing is a harder and less popular trip than its southern counterpart, but takes the keen tramper into a much less trammelled and wilder part of the range. Leslie Adkin, a Tararua enthusiast and founding member of the Levin-Waiopehu Tramping Club, was the first to complete a Northern Crossing in 1909. He and companion Bert Lancaster travelled up the Ohau River onto Dundas, crossed the Waiohine Pinnacles and Tarn Ridge, climbed Mitre and then descended along the Waingawa River. These days the most popular way to complete a Northern Crossing is still a traverse from the Ohau to the Waingawa, following part of Adkin's route across the Waiohine Pinnacles. However, a more direct route (as described here) starts from the Putara Road end in the Wairarapa, traverses the lumpy Dundas Ridge and then exits down past the new Waiopehu Hut.

This is a demanding trip, and parties tackling the tramp over the course of a normal weekend will probably need to reach Herepai Hut on the Friday night. Alternatively, it makes a splendid three-day trip.

From the Putara Road end a signposted track leads into forest and soon crosses the Mangatainoka River on a swingbridge. Travel up-valley is along a gentle track, until another swingbridge is crossed, when a steepish ascent ensues to a bush-covered knoll. Here, a signposted track junction indicates the way to Herepai Hut (the other branch leads to Roaring Stag Lodge). Head right to Herepai, along a gentle downsloping ridge to a small dip. Herepai Hut is ten minutes' walk up the other side of the dip and is positioned on the bushline with imposing views of the circle of peaks ahead: Herepai, Ruapae and East Peak.

After a well-deserved break at the hut, continue, following a track that ascends through subalpine scrub. The route becomes less defined as you climb, and the first real knob gained is Herepai. A small white cross (one of several encountered on the trip) lies just off the top and is inscribed with the name Stan Evans.

From here to Dundas Ridge, the track involves a considerable amount of up and down, with the trail barely defined in places. Indeed, it's very much a tactile experience, with the occasional gentle caress of leatherwood and travel through the tall tussocks conducted more by feel than sight. There are no poles and few cairns on the route, and in mist it can be a navigational challenge, especially in the reverse direction.

Nevertheless, on a clear day there are vistas of both the Manawatu and Wairarapa, and even the South Island and the distant peaks of Ruapehu and Taranaki can be visible. The next knob reached is Ruapae, which leads to a climb up East Peak. Here, the route turns sharply westwards, where a nasty, unwelcome 210 metre descent drops to a scrubby gap. This gap deserves the name of Hells Gate far more than that on the Southern Crossing, especially as a climb of almost the same height ensues up the other side to West Peak. The route changes direction abruptly once again on West Peak, striking southwest.

Late evening over Walker, West Peak and East Peak from Pukemoremore, Dundas Ridge

By this stage you're on Dundas Ridge, classic Tararua tops with some craggy peaks, few tarns and more than a little up and down travel. While it's fairly flat as far as Walker, Pukemoremore presents another climb, and by the time you reach the turn-off to Dundas Hut – marked by several cairns – you'll be feeling the effects of a

big day's efforts. The tidy, six-bunk hut lies on a spur to the east and is reached after a 15-minute descent off the main range. It makes a pleasant place to pass the night.

Back up on the ridge, more undulating travel follows, with a gradual climb to Logan, then a more significant climb to Dundas (1500 metres), whose top is covered with a large trig station. From a knob just southwest of Dundas, an unmarked and unmaintained route descends to the Mangahao Valley over Triangle Knob, presenting a possible bad-weather escape route off the tops.

Beyond Dundas, travel proves mostly undulating. About 30 metres below the top of Pt 1434, sidle left to a narrow cairned track leading across rock and tussock faces to Arete Biv.

The biv commands one of the best 'tops' positions of any hut in the Tararuas, and the small red shelter seems fittingly tiny in the gold tussock landscape. From the hut, the nearby Twins and Bannister look rather fearsome, while Mitre, Girdlestone and Brockett form significant summits to the southeast. As it can be quite damp, Arete Biv has no mattresses and even the hut book is waterproof!

Some people experience difficulty in finding Arete Biv during a storm, but there is a series of marker poles across a shelf south of the hut, that can be intercepted if

Gentians – one of the last alpines to flower in summer

you are travelling in the opposite direction. Follow these around to a sizeable tarn, then climb tussock slopes up to the summit of Arete (1505 metres). This and the next peak, Pukematawai, are interesting because together they lie at the head of virtually all of the major Tararua rivers: the Waiohine, Waingawa, Mangahao, Otaki and Ruamahanga. There are good views from here of the U-shaped Park valley, which Leslie Adkin first proposed had glacial origins. While the Park's profile certainly seems to suggest that glaciers did shape it, a lack of moraines normally associated with glaciation leads to some doubts about the theory.

There's a track junction just southeast of Pukematawai, marked by several poles, where the main range route continues. Instead, head right here onto a prominent spur that forms a crooked route to the scrubline, past an unmarked turn-off to Girdlestone Saddle and eventually to Te Matawai Hut. This rather unusual hut, with a ridiculously high ceiling, seems to be a tribute to the worst of 1970s architecture, but it's tidy enough and has a comfortable bunkroom.

The final leg of the tramp follows a prominent largely forested ridge over the summits of Richards Knob (past the Gable End Ridge turn-off), Twin Peak (where there's a trig and another cross), and finally Waiopehu. While you can see over the scrub that grows on these knobs, they are no longer covered in a field of *Celmisia spectabilis* daisies that were photographed by Adkin early in the 20th century – perhaps this is a sign of higher bushlines.

A short distance down from the summit of Waiopehu, just through a small patch of beech forest, is the new Waiopehu Hut, built in March/April 2002 and sporting panoramic views over the Manawatu. It replaces the old Waiopehu Hut, now removed, which was located a short distance down the ridge.

The final romp down the ridge passes through beech forest at first, then kamahi-tawa-podocarp forest with some extensive sections of tree ferns. It's further than you might expect and can be muddy, but eventually you reach farmland, from where it's a flat stroll to the carpark on Poads Road. By the end you'll be feeling the effects – and satisfaction – of having crossed the Tararua Range.

Tramper heading from Ruapae to East Peak

Mangahao Flats

Duration: 2 days.

Grade: Medium.

Times: Mangahao No. 1 Reservoir to Harris Creek bridge: 2.5–3 hours. Harris Creek bridge to Mangahao Flats Hut (16 bunks, wood stove, Category 3): 2 hours. Mangahao Flats to Girdlestone Saddle: 3 hours. Girdlestone Saddle to South Ohau River: 1–2 hours. South Ohau River to Poads Road: 3–4 hours.

Maps: S25 Levin, Tararua Forest Park Map.

Access: Turn off SH57 at Shannon onto Mangahao Road and follow this until its end at the Mangahao No. 1 Reservoir and dam. It's a long, narrow, winding, metalled road.

Alternative routes: For those who want to go only as far as Mangahao Flats and back, it's possible to end the tramp slightly differently. Downstream of Harris Creek Hut, travel up Dick Creek, over a small bush saddle, and then down Baber Creek, to emerge on the Puketurua Track, which ends at the far side of the dam. This is, however, off-track travel and is classed as medium–hard.

Information: DoC Waikanae, Ph 04 296 1112.

The Mangahao is undoubtedly one of the most attractive rivers in Tararua Forest Park, and a tramp to Mangahao Flats Hut provides a good weekend trip for families or for less experienced trampers. From the head of the Mangahao, it's also possible for more experienced trampers to continue over Girdlestone Saddle into the Ohau catchment.

After the long drive in from Shannon, you're more than ready to get out and stretch your legs. There's an impressive dam here, one of the earliest ones built in the country. Suggestions that the Mangahao had potential for generating hydro-electricity were mooted as far back as 1911, and the resultant dams were completed in

1924. Until recently, much of the reservoir was filled with the ugly stumps of trees that were drowned when the valley was flooded, but these have since been removed, and the area is more appealing as a result.

Tramper overlooks pool in Mangahao River

The track starts right from the reservoir edge and immediately plunges into bush, crossing a swing-bridge over an unnamed creek after ten minutes. However, when the reservoir is not full, it's often easier to sidle around its silty edge.

On a fine day when river levels are normal, parties may wish to avoid the track altogether and instead amble up-river. The track itself – typically for a Tararua valley sidle – has considerable up and down, especially in the first section to Harris Creek. In contrast, boulder-hopping along the river proves a delight, with frequent opportunities for swimming in deep green pools. After about an hour you reach a swingbridge, where the track crosses to the true right of the valley.

If you are following the river, there's a section of gorge travel upstream of the bridge. While this is not difficult, you will need to swim in a few very deep pools unless you scramble around in the bush. Be aware, however, that floods can change this section of river considerably, and if you are in any doubt it's best to stick to the track. After crossing Dick Creek, the track follows bush terraces for ten minutes to emerge at Harris Creek. The old Harris Creek Hut that had existed here since 1977 was removed in 2003. Up-valley there is good river travel once again as far as Mangahao Flats, making a dry weather alternative to the track.

The track from the Harris Creek bridge is also fairly pleasant, with considerably less up and down than the previous section. Thirty minutes later you reach the other major sidestream in the valley, the Barra. In flood, the Barra often used to be impassable, but in 2003 DoC erected a new bridge here, making the entire route as far as Mangahao Flats Hut an all-weather track.

Beyond Barra Creek, the track crosses a slip, where there are clear views over the Mangahao River as it curls around a substantial horseshoe bend. Not far beyond, you reach Mangahao Flats Hut on a bush terrace above the river. The large, roomy, 16-bunk hut was built in 1992 as a replacement for the old Avalanche Flats Hut, now removed.

After a night at Mangahao Flats Hut, some parties choose simply to walk back down the valley, but those who have made suitable transport arrangements can opt instead to continue into the Ohau Valley over Girdlestone Saddle. This section, however, is more difficult and can only be achieved when river levels are low. From the hut, a track continues up-valley on the true right. It passes through a couple of interesting 'frost flats' where stunted manuka grows, while further up are some larger grassy flats ideal for camping.

The track eventually crosses the Mangahao at a prominent river fork, then sidles through beech forest for ten minutes. Once over a stream it begins the short five-minute climb to Girdlestone Saddle and a track intersection. One track leads off up a bush spur towards Te Matawai Hut, while the other heads across the saddle down to the South Ohau River. Unless wet weather threatens, take the latter option, which soon drops into a small, steep creek. A violent flood has severely damaged this creek, and you'll need to do a bit of scrambling over loose rock and log debris. This doesn't last long, however, before a well-marked sidle track takes you out of the creek on the true left to bypass Dowling Falls.

The track soon deposits you in the South Ohau River, which you follow downstream to the junction with Butchers Stream. Note that the old South Ohau Hut that used to exist here was removed in 2003 after flood damage undermined its foundations. Travel down the Ohau from this point proves fairly straightforward, despite the gorge marked on the map – in recent years this has been substantially filled in with gravel from floods. It takes a further one-and-a-half hours to reach the confluence with the North Ohau River.

After a further half-hour in the river, a well-benched track starts on the true left. It passes the site of the old Ohau Shelter (which is now a good camping spot) then crosses a footbridge and sidles down valley. By this stage the forest is almost

Dragonfly, Ohau valley

subtropical, with nikau palms, mahoe, kiekie vines and dense tangles of supplejack, through which the track passes on an easy gradient. After crossing another footbridge you emerge suddenly onto farmland, from where it's a 15-minute walk to the carpark on Poads Road.

Mitre Flats

TARARUA FOREST PARK, WAIRARAPA

Duration: 2–3 days.

Grade: Medium.

Times: Upper Waingawa Road to Mitre Flats Hut (20 bunks, wood stove, gas rings, Category 2): 3–4 hours. Mitre Flats Hut to Mitre: ascent 3 hours; descent 2 hours.

Maps: S26 Carterton, S25 Levin, Tararua Forest Park Map.

Access: Turn off the SH2 Masterton bypass onto Upper Plain Road and follow this for some 10 km before turning left onto Upper Waingawa Road. There's an area to park your car at the farm roadend, known as 'The Pines'.

Alternative routes: From the summit of Mitre, it's possible to traverse Girdlestone and the Kings, then drop down over Baldy back to Mitre Flats Hut. This is, however, a very long day suitable only for experienced trampers, and the track down from Baldy has long been overgrown.

Information: DoC Masterton, Ph 06 377 0022.

The Waingawa is one the principal rivers of the eastern side of the Tararua Range, draining the slopes of the highest peak in the park, Mitre. At 1571 metres, Mitre is hardly a giant – even by North Island standards – but the tramp to the top is worthwhile, with some good views and a comfortable hut en route.

From 'The Pines', follow a 4WD farm track for some distance, to where poles lead down onto river terraces of the Waingawa. Shortly afterwards, a track starts through regenerating bush and finally leads into mature forest at the boundary of Tararua Forest Park. You are now on the benched Barra Track, named after Tararua veteran Bert Barra, who was something of a local hunting legend and who spent his last days living in a hut overlooking the Waingawa River. In places the track sidles quite high above the river, although you're often within earshot of it rushing through gorges below. The forest is a combination of rimu, kamahi and supplejack with some beech, and at its densest these form quite a dark canopy over the trail. During summer, the northern rata flowers spectacularly, a tribute to DoC's ongoing possum control in the area.

Several viewpoints open out, mainly of the river, but on one occasion you can see Jumbo and even Jumbo Hut. Later comes a view of Mitre itself. Don't be fooled by your first glimpse of Mitre Flats and the hut – there's still some distance to go as the track climbs steeply to avoid a large slip, then drops to cross the river over a suspension bridge.

The current 20-bunk hut (completed in 1988) is the third that has occupied Mitre Flats; the original was built in 1933 from timber cut on site and iron cladding carried in on horseback. The second hut, constructed in 1953 by the Masterton YMCA, required two loads of materials to be lugged in as, heartbreakingly, the first load was

Tramper on Peggy's Peak, Tararua Forest Park

mostly washed away in one of the Waingawa's notorious floods. Although today's hut is a pleasant and popular place to spend the night, those who prefer camping can find plenty of secluded spots on the northern end of the flats.

The track to Mitre starts near the hut, at first climbing stiffly onto a ridge, from where the gradient eases. Then it's a steady uphill plod, surprisingly without any really steep sections. Initially there's a rich understorey of kidney ferns beneath a canopy of rimu, miro and kamahi, but these later lapse into silver beech. Typically for the Tararuas, the silver beech becomes more and more stunted as you gain altitude, often forming exquisitely twisted shapes, until finally a band of leatherwood takes over. Above the scrub band, rock cairns lead ever upwards over tussock and scree slopes, and there are increasingly good views of the Kings, Baldy and the upper reaches of the Waingawa. The first summit reached is Peggy's Peak, which is separated from nearby Mitre by just a short and narrow stretch of ridge. Fortunately, the often strong winds that blow here come mainly from the west, thus pushing you away from a steep drop-off overhanging the South Mitre Stream.

South Mitre Stream, Tararua Forest Park

A large cairn marks the summit of Mitre, the top of the Tararuas, which is flat enough to support several tramping parties at once. There are views of Dundas Ridge and the spectacularly nasty-looking Bannister to the north, undulating Tarn Ridge to the northwest, and endless other forested slopes surrounding them. Even Kapiti Island is sometimes visible, far off in the haze.

The descent back to Mitre Flats is surprisingly non-jarring for a 1200 metre drop, mainly because the ridge reclines at such an even gradient. It's perfectly feasible to climb Mitre and walk back out in one day, but if there's no hurry another night at Mitre Flats could be pleasant. An extra day allows you time to follow the river back to the carpark. Although there are several gorges along the way, there is only one real significant swim near the end, and that can be avoided by scrambling out on the true left bank to rejoin the track.

Holdsworth • Jumbo

Duration: 2 days.

Grade: Medium.

Times: Holdsworth Lodge to Powell Hut (32 bunks, gas rings and heater, Category 2): 3–4 hours. Powell to Jumbo Hut (20 bunks, gas rings, wood stove, Category 2): 2.5–3.5 hours. Jumbo to Atiwhakatu Hut (8 bunks, open fire, Category 3): 1.5 hours. Atiwhakatu to Holdsworth Lodge: 2–3 hours.

Maps: S26 Carterton, S25 Levin, Tararua Forest Park Map.

Access: From SH2, just south of Masterton, turn onto Norfolk Road; this eventually becomes Mt Holdsworth Road. At the end of the road is a large carpark, toilets and Holdsworth Lodge (which is available for overnight stays).

Alternative routes: If the weather is bad, it's possible to drop off the ridge north of Mt Holdsworth along a spur known as the East Holdsworth Ridge. This joins the Atiwhakatu Valley track at the Holdsworth Creek confluence.

Information: DoC Masterton, Ph 06 377 0022.

This route – up to Powell Hut and Mt Holdsworth, then across the tops to Jumbo Hut, and finally down the Atiwhakatu Valley – forms one of the classic Tararua weekend tramps, with the bonus that it is a tidy round trip. It's enjoyable no matter what the time of year, but be warned: on weekends and during summer, expect crowds! Powell Hut has, for some years, been the most popular hut in the park and regularly gets full. Although this is classed as a medium trip, the tops – like most of those in the Tararuas – are extremely exposed and can be lethal for ill-equipped or inexperienced parties during bad weather.

From Holdsworth Lodge (where there is an intentions book) a gravelled track heads up-valley, soon crossing the Atiwhakatu River on a sizeable footbridge. Shortly afterwards, the track forks; head left here up the well-benched and gravelled Gentle Annie Track, which has been upgraded in recent years. At first, some Tararua stalwarts bemoaned these improvements, but in reality a track as popular as this one needs a fairly hardened surface if it is to avoid becoming severely eroded. As you climb, the vegetation changes gradually from a mix of the more lush podocarp-broadleaf-beech forest to one that is increasingly dominated by beech, mainly silver.

Silver beech forest, Mt Holdsworth

After steady upwards progress, a flatter section of the track leads onto a viewpoint at Rocky Lookout. More undulating ridge travel ensues, until you reach a prominent junction where a track branches off down to Totara Flats. Keep going upwards, until a flat respite comes across Pig Flat. Shortly past the flat you reach Mountain House, a shelter built by the Wellington Tramping and Mountaineering Club to replace the old Mountain House Hut.

Beyond the shelter, the track steepens for the final push to Powell Hut, which sits on the bushline. This modern, large, well-designed hut was officially opened in 2000, the most recent in a succession of Powell Huts dating back to 1939. Previous versions were reputedly haunted by 'Cedric the Ghost', thought to be the spirit of hunter Cedric Wilson, who died near Mitre during 1945. It's not yet known whether Cedric has taken up residence in the new hut.

With its commanding views over the Wairarapa plains and the Atiwhakatu Valley, the verandah of Powell Hut is a fine place to watch the last of the day's light fade, followed later by the twinkling emergence of both the stars and the lights of Masterton. Above Powell Hut, a well-worn (but not poled) route leads up to Mt Holdsworth (1470 metres), the most popular summit in the Tararua Range. A trig station marks the top, which – more often than not – is shrouded in cloud.

Drop down onto the ridge leading north to Jumbo in the direction indicated by the signpost. The well-traipsed tops here are pretty easy going by Tararua standards, dropping steadily to a low saddle and then beginning a climb up past a tarn towards the angular summit of Jumbo. On a good day there are views of the Broken Axe Pinnacles, McGregor and Baldy. On top, a signpost indicates the correct spur to follow down to Jumbo Hut. Like Powell, Jumbo Hut also commands a fine position on the bushline, with extensive views eastwards.

A well-marked track leads from Jumbo Hut down into the Atiwhakatu Valley on what is called 'Rain Gauge Spur' – a once unofficial route (starting beyond the rain gauge) that is now more popular than the older track further north. After a sharp descent, the track reaches the Atiwhakatu River just upstream of Atiwhakatu Hut.

From the hut you head downstream on a well-benched and graded track – a far cry from the rough old route that used to exist. Now that all the major side-streams have been bridged, this is an all-weather track. Fast travel leads onto Holdsworth Creek, spanned by a swingbridge, while the track beyond to Donnelly Flat passes some good viewpoints of the river. There are camping spots at Donnelly Flat, complete with permanent fireplaces. From here it's simply a matter of ambling back out to Holdsworth Lodge.

The new Powell Hut, Mt Holdsworth

Southern Crossing

Duration: 2–3 days.

Grade: Medium–Hard.

Times: Otaki Forks to Field Hut (15 bunks, wood stove, Category 3): 2–3 hours. Field to Kime Hut (32 bunks, no mattresses, Category 3): 2–3 hours. Kime to Alpha Hut (20 bunks, wood stove, Category 3): 4–5 hours. Alpha to Kaitoke via Marchant Ridge: 6–8 hours; via Tauherenikau Valley and Smith Creek: 7–8 hours.

Maps: S26 Carterton, Tararua Forest Park Map.

Access: Just south of Otaki, turn off SH1 onto Otaki Gorge Road. At the end of the road is a large carpark, plus toilets, a caretaker's residence and access to Parawai Lodge. Owing to vandalism, it is not recommended that you park a car overnight at the Kaitoke end.

Alternative routes: From Alpha Hut it's possible to complete the more traditional Southern Crossing over Bull Mound to Cone Hut and from there to the roadend at Walls Whare.

Information: DoC Waikanae, Ph 04 296 1112.

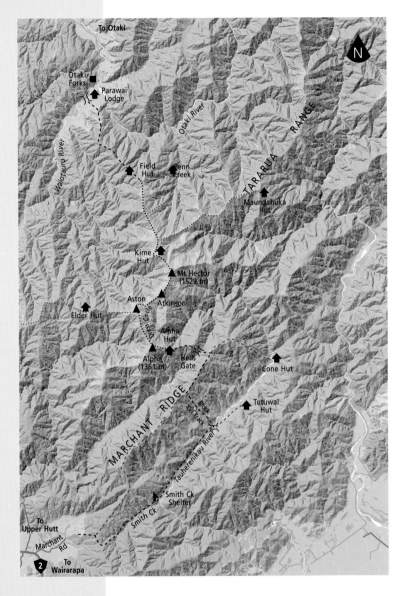

Perhaps *the* classic Tararua tramp is Southern Crossing. It's a track with a long history, preceding even the formation of New Zealand's first tramping club, the Tararua Tramping Club, in 1919. The idea for what later became known as the Southern Crossing originated with the Mt Hector Track Committee, a group that sought to develop a tourist track in the southern Tararuas during the first part of the 20th century. The group erected three huts: Alpha (built in 1915 and the first alpine hut in the Tararua Range), Top Tauherenikau (built in 1917) and Te Moemoea Hut (built in 1919 near Otaki Forks).

The original Southern Crossing route used to finish (or begin) at Walls Whare, near Greytown, but most parties now opt to end at Kaitoke, near Upper Hutt. It's somewhat ironic that this route is not actually a crossing and does in fact start and finish on the western side of the Tararua Range. That said, ending at Kaitoke allows for somewhat easier transport arrangements, particularly for Wellington trampers.

The starting point, Otaki Forks, lies at the junction of several rivers and tracks, and forms a popular area for camping and picnicking as well as tramping. From the overnight parking area, a short track leads down to a picnic area and a large wooden bridge over the Waiotauru River. Across the bridge, a brief climb leads to a grassy river terrace and a junction with the track to Waitewaewae. Take the track signposted to Field Hut. A long but not particularly strenuous ascent ensues.

The track initially passes through regenerating scrub, then soon enters more mature forest where kamahi and hinau dominate, along with the occasional totara. Typically for the Tararuas, silver beech takes over higher up. Further on, you reach Field Hut, the oldest-surviving hut in the park. Commissioned by the Tararua Tramping Club and completed in 1924, Field Hut was built out of timber pit-sawn on site by master bushman Joe Gibbs. Although the hut has changed extensively since then, it's still just as welcome today as it must have been for those early trampers. Many parties opt to walk this far on their first night, in order to break up the long climb to Kime Hut.

View from Field Peak of the Beehives, Southern Crossing

Above Field Hut and after a brief climb through subalpine scrub, you reach the aptly named Table Top – a flat expanse of tops now partially boardwalked. As is usual on Tararua tops, there are very few poles, but the track is certainly well-defined from years of use. A few sections sidle, but mostly the route just heads uphill. Botanically,

Kime Hut, Southern Crossing

the area proves quite lush, with gentians, North Island edelweiss, several *Celmisia* species and the attractive but uncharacteristically soft-spined Tararua speargrass. Near the top, some waratahs appear, and shortly after comes the signpost indicating the turn-off to Bridge Peak and Maungahuka Hut. Not far from here, just over the gentle rise of Hut Mound, Kime Hut lies nestled in a shallow dip by a prominent tarn.

Due to its large size and high ceiling, Kime can be a cold hut, and – as often as not – the weather is bleak. However, the hut has recently had new mattresses installed, making it more comfortable than it used to be. From here you embark across an exposed section of tops to Alpha Hut. Initially, the track climbs to Field Peak, then drops sharply to a saddle and climbs again to Mt Hector, at 1529 metres the highest point on the crossing.

On a good day, Mt Hector provides a remarkable viewpoint, with mountains as distant as the Inland Kaikoura Range sometimes visible. Marking the summit is a substantial wooden memorial cross, built to commemorate trampers and climbers who lost their lives in both world wars. In winter, windblown sastrugi-like ice sometimes lends it more the appearance of a memorial to Antarctic explorers.

From Mt Hector the route heads almost directly south, dropping to a shallow saddle, before climbing over the mounds known as The Beehives. The narrowest section of the entire route ensues, one that could potentially be dangerous in high winds or winter conditions.

Beyond, undulating tops travel leads to Atkinson, which is marked by a short waratah. Past Pt 1372 the terrain becomes very flat and almost moorlike, but the track is so well-defined that it would be difficult to come off it anywhere – except, of course, when it lies under a covering of snow. From Aston, the track starts curling southeast, around the Dress Circle and then begins a climb onto Alpha, where it swings directly east. On a good day, Alpha affords perhaps the best vantage point of the crossing, with views back around the sweep of the Dress Circle and over the extensive forests of the neighbouring Tauherenikau and Hutt catchments.

A steady plod from Alpha takes you once more down into forest, from where it's a pleasant stroll through wonderfully stunted silver beech to Alpha Hut. This version is the third Alpha, built in 1983. Beyond Alpha, a forested track leads towards the Marchant Ridge and a choice of routes out. After passing Hells Gate (a small dip in the bush ridge with an exaggerated name) you reach a track junction. The left branch would take you over Bull Mound and out to Walls Whare via Mt Reeves – the traditional Southern Crossing route. Instead, head right here, over Omega, and continue along the undulating forest of Marchant Ridge until you reach the signposted junction with the Block XVI Track.

There's another choice of routes here: either the fairly tedious up-and-down of the deceptively long Marchant Ridge; or the option that it is preferred by many, out through the Tauherenikau Valley via the Block XVI Track. (Both routes eventually rejoin near the track end at Kaitoke.) The latter does involve a 300-metre descent, but once you are down in the Tauherenikau valley, travel is generally flat and easygoing on forested river terraces that are dominated by extensive stands of rimu. At Smith Creek Shelter, an agreeably shady and well-benched track ascends gradually beside Smith Creek, broken only by one scramble around an area of recent slips. Near the head of Smith Creek, the track climbs more sharply over a saddle of regenerating forest to begin a sidle towards Kaitoke, passing the Marchant Ridge track en route. At the end of the tramp you will feel that you have really covered some ground – which you have. It's somewhat deflating then, to hear that the fastest time for completing the annual run along the entire Southern Crossing is an astonishing four hours and 20 minutes!

The Southern Crossing from lower slopes of Alpha

Mt Matthews

Duration: 1–2 days.

Grade: Medium.

Times: Visitor centre to Turere bridge: 1.5–2 hours. Orongorongo River to Baine Hut: 1 hour. Baine Hut to Mt Matthews: 2–3 hours each way.

Maps: R27/28 Wellington, Rimutaka/Haurangi Forest Park map.

Access: From Wellington, drive to Wainuiomata, then head south along the Coast Road. After about 10 km a signpost indicates the turn-off to the Catchpool Valley, visitor centre and roadend.

Alternative routes: An alternative route up Mt Matthews can be made from the Wairarapa side, up Mukamuka Stream onto the South Saddle, and then up to the summit itself. Access for this route is from Palliser Bay, west of Lake Ferry.

Information: Catchpool Visitor Centre, Ph 04 564 8551; DOC Wellington Info Centre, Ph 04 472 7356.

Huts/camps: Jans, Raukawa and Oaks Huts can all be booked through the Catchpool Visitor Centre. Camping is possible at several sites in the Orongorongo valley (at Manuka Flat and Big Bend) and near Matthews Stream.

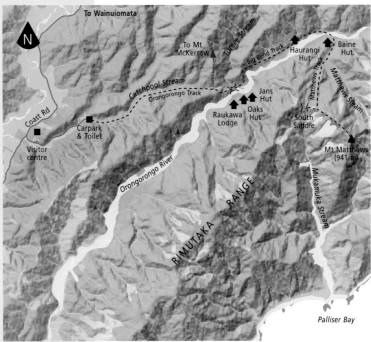

The relatively low, but deceptively rugged, Rimutakas are the southernmost range along the North Island's mountain spine, which extends from East Cape to Wellington. Ascending Mt Matthews, which at 941 metres is the highest peak in the range, can be accomplished over a weekend, or if you're really keen, in as little as one day.

Access to the peak begins beside one of the country's most popular walks, the Orongorongo Track. This track departs from a parking area in the Catchpool valley, beyond a visitor centre where there is information and a small shop.

The gentle gradient of the Orongorongo Track passes through pine trees at first, then heads into a semi-tropical grove where nikau palms and kiekie vines are conspicuous, before breaking out into a more open area of red beech forest. Later, there are pockets of rimu, miro and kamahi. Attractive information panels provide details of the area's ecology. After about five kilometres, the track descends to an arched bridge over the

Turere Stream and finally into the gravelly expanse of the Orongorongo River itself. The Orongorongo is the largest watercourse in the park and runs southward to meet Cook Strait on the coastline separating Wellington from the Wairarapa.

There are several DoC-managed huts in the valley, which due to their popularity must be pre-booked. Numerous private huts also lie tucked away in the bush, dating back to the days before the formation of the Rimutaka Forest Park, when the valley was a popular spot for Wellingtonians to build holiday baches. The track to Mt Matthews takes you some three kilometres upstream, either on the Big Bend Track on the true right of the valley, or – if water levels are low – on the faster route along the riverbed.

There are good views of the range from the open riverbed, although Mt Matthews as yet remains hidden. Emergent above the forest are numerous northern rata trees, many of which sadly have been devastated by possums, first introduced to New Zealand in the Rimutaka Range in 1893. With such a long history of being browsed, the Rimutaka forests have very visible scars. Erosion remains prominent, both from goat browsing and the devastation wrought by the 1968 storm that sank the *Wahine*.

After an hour's walk up-valley you reach a signpost indicating the start of the Mt Matthews track. The route initially pushes through *Buddleia*, an introduced plant that has become a problem weed in open riverbeds like the Orongorongo, but soon you reach native forest and the small clearing where the Hutt Valley Tramping Club's Baine Hut (locked) is situated. Beyond, the track leads to Matthews Stream, crossing it a few times and passing a couple of campsites.

If you have any doubts about the power of the Earth to thrust mountains up along geological faults, the next section of track soon dispels them. Typical of mountain ranges in the North Island, the Rimutaka Range is composed chiefly of greywacke and

Orongorongo valley, Rimutaka Range beyond

has been uplifted over the last 12 million years. Much of this uplift has occurred slowly, at the rate of a few centimetres per year, but on occasions severe earthquakes have made dramatic upthrusts. The last major local earthquake occurred in 1855, measured about 8.0 on the Richter scale and raised the Rimutaka Range by approximately three metres. Some of the large eroded scars on the range were also caused by the quake. Over this landscape, the track climbs very steeply through open beech forest then it sidles across a bushcovered knob before reaching a signpost. Here the side-track leads to the South Saddle branches off.

Silver beech forest, Rimutaka Range

The main track leads uphill again, and after a breathless ascent it emerges onto a grassy plateau. Impressive views unfold westwards of Wellington Harbour and the surrounding hills, while to the east you can hear the pounding surf of Palliser Bay.

The last section of the climb leads up a very steep face, onto a narrow section of ridge cloaked in silver beech forest. The trees form uniform stands here as well as in the Tararua Range further north, and are often gnarled and heavily mossclad. Through this forest a deceptively long (though well-marked) route leads along the ridge, dipping down to the right at one point, before finally reaching Mt Matthews itself. Disappointingly (for the views), the summit is forest-clad, but gaps in the trees allow glimpses of the long curve of Palliser Bay and of the Wairarapa plains below.

The descent back to your camp needs to be done carefully to avoid wrenching your knees – hold on to the tree trunks to help brake your descent. Whiteheads and riflemen are common in these higher altitudes of the park, and during the descent you may see flocks of them flitting over branches in their search for insects.

Kapiti Island

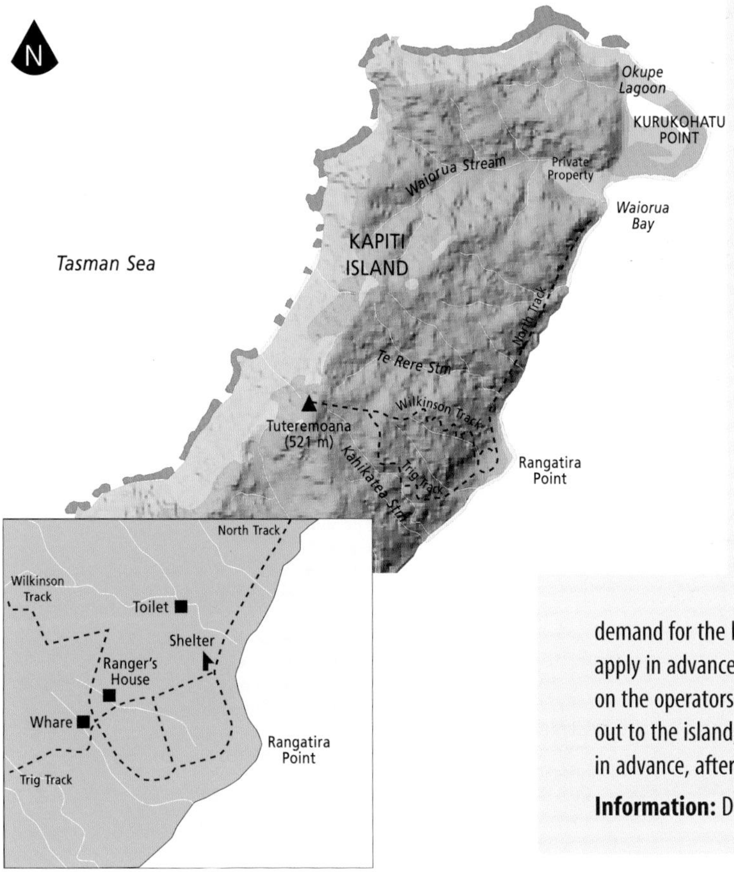

Duration: 1 day.

Grade: Easy.

Times: Rangatira Point to Tuteremoana Trig and return via Wilkinson and Trig Tracks: 3–4 hours. North Track to Okupe Lagoon: 2–3 hours return.

Map: R26 Paraparaumu.

Access: Kapiti Island is accessible from Paraparaumu Beach, off SH1 north of Wellington. To visit the island you must first obtain a permit from DoC in Wellington ($9 for adults, $4.50 for children). During summer months and at weekends there is heavy demand for the limited number of permits, so apply in advance. DoC can also provide information on the operators who are licensed to run boat trips out to the island; these trips must also be booked in advance, after you have received your permit.

Information: DoC Wellington, Ph 04 472 7356.

Kapiti Island lies five kilometres west of Paraparaumu, making it the most accessible nature Reserve in the country. Visitors to the DoC-managed island are often over-whelmed at the abundance of wildlife, especially the chance to see rare native birds such as takahe, kokako, saddlebacks, weka and stitchbirds. Some of the more common birds that abound on Kapiti include kaka, tui, bellbirds, robins, wood pigeons and pukeko.

The island is separated from the mainland by a 20-minute launch ride. Visitors disembark at the stony beach at Rangatira Point, the base for Kapiti's resident rangers. At the shelter here, you receive a brief introduction to the island – including information on current track conditions – and are then left to explore by yourself. The wildlife is certainly the main reason to visit – the experience of having a kaka land on your head or seeing a takahe strutting around are not easily forgotten – but there are some good day tramps on the island, and this can be an excellent way to view birds in a variety of habitats.

Two routes, the Wilkinson and Trig Tracks, both start from Rangatira Point near the site of the historic whare and climb through forest on the eastern slopes of the island. About three-quarters of the way up, the two meet to form a single track that leads to the top of the island, a point called Tuteremoana (521 metres). There's a viewing tower here with great vistas down the sheer cliffs on the island's western side and over to the Kapiti coast. Sometimes, on clear days, Mt Taranaki and the South Island are visible too. After spending some time on the summit, you can descend back to the junction and then take the alternative track to the one you ascended to make a partial round trip. As the Wilkinson Track has a more gradual gradient, it's probably the more pleasant to descend.

A third route, called the North Track, also starts from near Rangatira Point. From the north end of Rangatira Bay it climbs above the coastline, skirting high around some cliffs and then dropping back down closer to the shore. After this it largely follows the coast, with some undulations, before ending at Waiorua Bay. The low forest along this coast is particularly good for observing saddlebacks. There's an area of private Maori land in this northern part of the island, which can be avoided by walking along the shore to the north of the bay. From here a short stroll leads to Okupe Lagoon, a wetland popular with waterfowl.

Kapiti Island at dusk, seen from Paekakariki Beach

Most trips to Kapiti last from 9am to 3pm, which gives ample time for either walk. It is possible to tramp both the coastal and Tuteremoana tracks within this time, but you stand a better chance of encountering Kapiti's rarer birds if you spend some time in one spot as a passive observer.

The North Island saddleback, an ancient wattlebird now extinct on the mainland, is easily identified by the distinctive 'tiekie, tiekie' call described by its Maori name. Another wattlebird is the North Island kokako (introduced to the island in 1994), recognised by its grey plumage and bright blue wattles. Kokako have perhaps the most melodic of all birdcalls, certainly the most haunting.

European settlers once described stitchbirds, or hihi, as the most common bird in the New Zealand forest. To-day, however, they are found only on predator-free islands such as Kapiti, where they were introduced in the 1980s. Male stitchbirds are strikingly attractive, with yellow and black plumage, while the females have more earthy tones. Another of Kapiti's special inhabitants, the little spotted kiwi, was released on the island early in the 20th century. At around 1000 birds, the Kapiti population is the largest in the country – although, of course, because of their nocturnal habits you won't see or hear them.

Kapiti has only recently become such a paradise for native birds – as little as 100 years ago the island was, literally, a mess. Kiore, or Polynesian rats, were already well established on the island after earlier occupation by Maori, that included the famed and feared Ngati Toa war-

North Island kaka, Nestor meridionalis septentrionalis

rior, Te Rauparaha. From the 1820s to 1840s American whalers operated several bases on Kapiti Island, and the Norway rats that escaped from their ships were the first in a long succession of mammal introductions by Pakeha that were to further devastate the island's wildlife.

During the 1840s, several farms were established on Kapiti, and farmers burned and cleared over 75 per cent of the island's forest. In addition to cattle and sheep, the farmers brought goats, pigs, cats and dogs. As if the forests hadn't suffered enough already, in 1892 possums were also introduced. Farming on Kapiti soon proved marginal, and by the end of the 19th century it was largely abandoned.

During the 1890s, several people who had become dismayed at the escalating destruction of New Zealand's native forests and wildlife began advocating the potential of the island as a reserve. Finally, in 1897, Kapiti became New Zealand's third official nature reserve (after Resolution Island in Fiordland and the Hauraki Gulf's Little Barrier Island).

Through caretakers' efforts, wild goats, cats and dogs were exterminated from Kapiti in the first half of the 20th century, but it was not until 1986 that possums were finally eradicated from the island – the culmination of a six-year military-style operation. Since the removal of possums the island's vegetation has responded well, with kohekohe, northern rata and other possum-palatable plants recovering spectacularly. Rats proved a more persistent problem, hampering in particular the breeding efforts of stitchbirds and saddlebacks. However, in 1996 DoC successfully eradicated these, the last of Kapiti's pests, using rat bait sown from a helicopter. Since then there have been encouraging signs of the island's further recovery – for example, sightings of native lizard species are increasing – and it is hoped that breeding by saddlebacks and stitchbirds will increase correspondingly.

Kapiti's transformation from ravaged farmland to island sanctuary is quite extraordinary. The birdlife on the island now provides not only a sober reminder of what tramping on the New Zealand mainland was like not so long ago, but also an insight into what can be achieved through the ongoing efforts of DoC, conservation groups and volunteers. It's a symbol of hope for the future.

Takahe, Porphyrio mantelli, *Kapiti Island Nature Reserve*